ARCHITECTURE AT THE INTERVAL

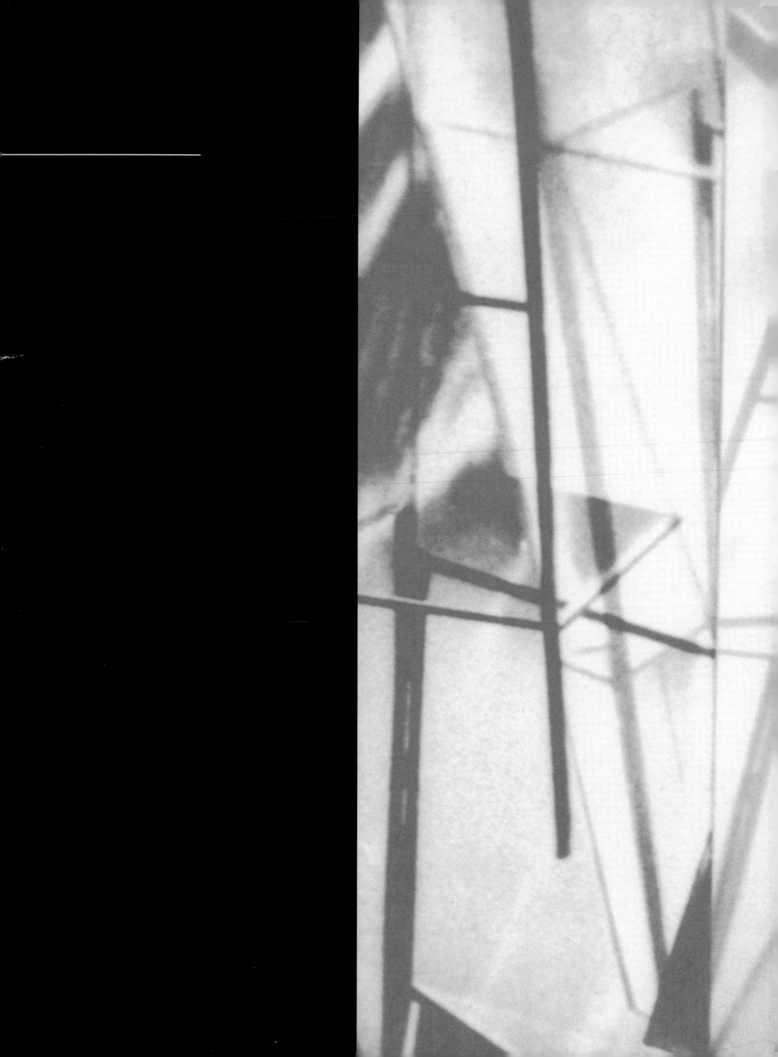

ASYMPTOTE

HANI   LISE ANNE
RASHID + COUTURE

ARCHITECTURE AT THE INTERVAL

RIZZOLI
NEW YORK

This book is dedicated to the many people
who over the past few years have contributed their energy and inspiration to this
body of work. We would especially like to
thank the dedicated assistants listed on the
closing page of this book, and our families,
who provide unfailing support. The community of architects, artists, theoreticians, and
friends that we have been fortunate to know
and be inspired by include, among others:
Allan Chasanoff, Thomas Leeser, Lebbeus
Woods, Mark Wigley, Elizabeth Diller, Eytan
Kaufman, Daniel Libeskind, Wolf Prix,
Frédéric Migayrou, Silvia Dainese, Bernard
Tschumi, Steven Holl, Michael Sorkin, Laurel
Wilson, Susana Torre, Michael Rotondi,
Quentin Vandoosselaere, Peter Cook, and
Vito Acconci.

First published in the United States of America in 1995
by Rizzoli International Publications, Inc.
300 Park Avenue South, New York, NY 10010

Copyright © 1995 Rizzoli International Publications, Inc.
and Asymptote Architecture

Library of Congress Cataloging-in-Publication Data

Rashid, Hani, 1958–
Asymptote : architecture at the interval / by Hani Rashid and Lise
Anne Couture.
p.   cm.
ISBN 0–8478–1861–6
1. Asymptote (Firm) 2. Architecture, Postmodern—United States.
3. Architecture—Competitions—United States.   I. Couture,
Lise Anne, 1959– . II. Title.
NA737.A83R37 1995   94-45009
720'.92'2—dc20   CIP

Cover: Hyperfine Splitting 006 © Asymptote Architecture

Designed by Asymptote
Printed and bound in Singapore

CONTENTS

Today ever-expanding thresholds of speed, efficiency, and meaning are changing our definitions of city space in completely unpredictable ways, and by extension challenging our understanding of architecture within the reconfigured polis. Traditional concerns with environment, behavior, function, and perfection no longer suffice as the limits according to which we design, theorize, and build architecture today.

Through its research Asymptote seeks to reexamine architecture's place within cultural practices that determine meaning, particularly within the realms of technology, media, telecommunications, and other spatiotemporal shifts marking the closing down of a millennium. The investigations (speculative writing, collage, drawing, installations, computer-generated images and environments, building designs, and urban planning proposals) traverse not only conventional notions of space, enclosure, and order, but also the fluctuating territories that define the post-information age.

To negotiate unknown terrain, navigators of the past depended on instruments of visualization that used descriptive geometry to configure space. From the astrolabe to the theodolite and transit; from the lighthouse to radar; from the camera obscura and photography to the electron microscope and digital imaging; or from Morse code to radio and television to the Internet, technological innovation has traditionally evolved as a result of humankind's unyielding desire to navigate the incomprehensible abyss.

With the invention of the printing press, ideas, methods, doctrines, and propaganda were issued with increased ease and efficiency. Prior to this critical cultural shift, building was a profound arbiter of meaning; in effect, a scaffold on which popes, merchants, and citizens assembled beliefs, mandates, morals, codes, and ethics.

The Enlightenment and positivist systems of thought introduced models of certainty seminal to the formation of modernity. Within these systems man held the central position, empowered by reason and entrenched in the endless acquisition of knowledge. Fabricated rules of geometry and constructed perspective inevitably transformed the discipline of architecture; now it was preoccupied with using material form to manifest transcendence.

By the early twentieth century the architect's long struggle against mathematical abstraction had merged with the discovery of innovative industrial and military technology, and new models of perfection were created. Modernism saw its salvation in the machine paradigm; ships, locomotives, factories, airplanes, and assembly lines embodied what was perceived as mystical precision. What higher ideal could architecture possibly emulate than the elegance of such models of ingenuity, efficiency, and hygiene?

During the Apollo mission in 1969 the technology of the lunar module was upstaged by its live broadcast on television, effectively bankrupting the modernist project. This event indisputably marked the full emergence of the post-information age. Information, image, speed, and media now would forever overshadow the prowess of the machine and the aura of the artifact. Today we find ourselves immersed in a spatiality in which indeterminate cultural identities merge with individual autonomy; borders become blurred and desires, transient. Today we navigate precariously according to these revised perceptions of space and meaning.

Architecture is not immune to these processes of mutation and distortion. Traveling between cities, sending a fax, channel surfing, computer hacking, teleconferencing, and telephone sex are all means by which we navigate space, time, and meaning today. Entirely new industries have emerged based on the acquisition and instant dissemination of information. These information-exchange mechanisms, such as CNN (Cable News Network) and global computer networks, undoubtedly are reconfiguring our comprehension of space.

Architecture for such fluid, dimensionless territories can only be an utterance, without language; a new architecture that is anticipatory, imperfect, and precisely misaligned.

8

Is there an architecture that does not retreat, an architectural work whose structure is not strengthened by distance? Distance from a grounding, codifying subject which, despite the recent history of its collapse, has not ceased to reassert itself, to recreate miasmas of non-objective spatiality. Is there an architecture liberated from permanence, where the event is not merely the advent of a new object?

Asymptote opposes coincidence to siting, installation to foundation, in order to claim an emphatic right to build unencumbered by the traditional spatial order imposed by a foundation. "Marinetti's locomotive has derailed," according to Hani Rashid in "On Recent Non-Events." The mobility and speed embraced by the Futurists have not, in the end, caused a radical change in how we conceive our relation to space. Only Laszlo Moholy-Nagy in "Vision in Motion" possibly under-stood that the proliferation of optical instruments in the twentieth century has introduced such a fragmentation of the visible that a demarcated position in space (*l'inscription spatiale*) is no longer assumed a permanent referent.

Asymptote proposes a reconfiguration of architecture through a radical mutation of its relation to space as an abstract referent, the one-dimensional space of geometry. Henceforth, architec-ture will organize material that is complex, perpetually over-determined, supported by permanent grafts and overlaps, deformed by use, and enhanced by ever-changing symbolic interpretations. The architectural work is no longer relative only to its spatial inscription, the reified structure of an establishment that imposed a hierarchic ordering upon all political, economic, and social parameters. Today architecture must organize itself into different configurations simultaneously, hybrid spatialities nourished by technology and media. As Hani Rashid and Lise Anne Couture assert, architecture is entering an age of fluidity without the ontological anchor that geometric-ally defined space previously supplied; it must express and create new modalities, open up pos-sible worlds.

How is building possible; or rather, how can we build the possible, simultaneously all possibles? With Asymptote the very idea of a deconstruction, of a permanent negotiation with the notion of origin, seems remote. The assertion of a generalized textuality, still apparent in the idea of Daniel Libeskind's Writing Machine project for the 1985 Venice Biennale, is detached from a direct link to space. In its break with traditional hermeneutics the "archi-text" (*archi-écriture*)—invariably conceived as a dyad, a spacing—retained its distance, a spatializing principle, the consequence of a resort to Kantian intuition. Asymptote definitively wrenches Libeskind's machine from its prespatial anchor, from this distance that reduces an architect's work to a game of displacement, to a permanent dislocation from its modern foundation. In its retreat the text as "trace" preserves, beyond the transcendental reduction of an empirical spatiality, a dif-ference linked as surely to space as to what it differentiates, yet it does not appear objectively spatial. This refocuses architecture's self-referentiality back on itself, attaches architecture to a particular outcome, an end that constantly orients the project toward its innate composition. This strictly Kantian approach dictates program, a complete series of temporal metaphors and procedures that determine construction.

To "program" Asymptote opposes a "diagnosis" that balances the constraints inherent in pro-gramming and reincorporates all the cultural values and uses that nourish context. Asymptote's Optigraph studies expose the phenomenal terrain as it truly is. The anthropocentric gaze no longer defines measure: measure based on Cartesian geometry is replaced by a multiplicity of "infinitesimal dimensions" at once spatial and qualitative, simulated or cathode images that are continuously overlaid onto our understanding of the urban realm or the private domain. The Optigraph renders legible what is already determined, what has meaning (*sens*), a "surveil-lance" that remains a sign. Asymptote's "degree zero" is no longer the tabula rasa of modernism but the factual basis of a pre-existing complexity in which program gives way to the axiomatic. Asymptote inverts the hierarchy between technologies and their capacity to deal with the real and considers every site of intervention a set of givens, a collection of information the architect must address and organize. History no longer follows the normative rule that constantly rele-gates architecture to the monumental; it turns against postmodern historicism, becoming mem-ory open to new operations. Architecture must work with the fact that linear time has been absorbed by technology that has introduced simultaneity, the immediacy of information, and the instantaneousness of the digital response.

In addition to program, it is the architectural method—that framework supported by models, norms, syntax, codification—that should be toppled. Asymptote discards the permanent revival of typologies, even the very question of typologies, as an ever-present matter of convention, "interminable vapors of convention, the purgatory of quality," as Hani Rashid writes. If Asymptote forcefully revives the modern question of foundation, of established ground, this never formally transpires into a form, a style, a strategy. Steel Cloud, a project in downtown Los Angeles, evokes Le Corbusier's masterplan for the center of Paris, or Ivan Leonidov's buildings, except that here there is no tabula rasa. The starting point is the physical image of displacement, an architecture already leaning toward mobility: the freeway above which the Steel Cloud project is to be constructed. If space remains one of the modalities of building it is never defined as an occupied site. The electronic instrument renders all notions of place reversible, and this reversibility reemerges most often in Asymptote's projects. The stages for the Moscow State Theater and Steel Cloud open to the city; the walls move to reveal the spectacle of the city, abolishing the exteriority of a performance space. A sculpture garden is laid out on elevated scaffolding, while gigantic aquariums mechanically recreate the ocean's movement. Detail and motif create images according to a reversed hierarchy: the library's information display screen becomes a billboard above the freeway; the cinemas are open to the air, like convertibles at a traditional American drive-in theater. Thus the projects monumentalize one's private emotional experience of the city and its details, definitively disrupting the hierarchy of forms and functions.

In the most direct sense the city already exists, permanently reinventing itself as an organization without exteriority, a "ready-made" city that must be accepted as the a priori of all architectural endeavors. For the Berlin Spreebogen competition Asymptote recycles everything constituting that city's intertextuality, from the former division created by the Berlin Wall to its historical axes. The Optigraph experiments, notably those made in Paris, move toward redefining the city, its unity, the very principle of its built presence. They confirm the city as the domain of complexity, an entangled mass of events that constitutes a permanent phenomenological ground, recovered topographies that no longer correspond to one another. Architecture no longer defines itself according to the reigning principle of identifying built form and construction as object. The formal unity of a building, the platonic shadow of a temple or villa, have always satisfied Enlightenment logic and modern rationality. As its own prerequisite Asymptote constantly posits a return to the surface of the palimpsest, to the permanently recovered utterances that constitute the reality of a city and exist alongside it.

The Alexandria Library presented Asymptote with enormous tension between the idea of foundation and cultural memory and a genuine, pragmatic program for a contemporary library. The library becomes a unique book whose contents are in perpetual motion, an open book continually reaffirmed through exchange, transference, the fragmentary multiplication of disciplines. It is architecture in which the structure's physical unity remains a vital sign. Asymptote takes origin and the territorial and cultural conditions that determine site and reincorporates these as dynamic rather than static aspects of the project, thus overthrowing its status as a timepiece and its relation to memory, to history. Memory fails to mobilize the theatrical force of the temporal; it has lost the unified stage presence conceded to it by the Renaissance.

"Amnesia" and "anemia" deny monumentality's static time, instead reclaiming presence, an infinite extension of the now (*maintenent*), the desire to rediscover the principle of ambivalent memory that Jacques Derrida emphasized in "Le puit et la pyramide." Building should be autonomous; this would not liberate it from the traditional constraints of architecture, but these no longer determine form or function. Asymptote's claim to autonomy is its capacity to specify all elements—symbolic, technical, and material—that could contribute to a project. "Autonomy" is not the modernist term of idealism or abstraction denounced by social critics. Autonomy is the desire to think and to labor within the entire complex sphere of the real. The architectural work becomes an unfinished object, a permanent continuum of projects that have reached the limits of definition, that are limited both in their ability to define themselves and to be defined socially, through use. The definition of a project's unity is its pragmatism, its ability to reconstruct its universal meaning for each one of us. There is a silence in architecture that is not the silence of an idealized form, an architectural "non-event," but an introduction to the eventual as something related to the event, the eventual that operates at the heart of building, affirming an architecture in action, perpetually renewed.

Frédéric Migayrou is the *Conseiller pour les Arts Plastiques* with the French Ministry of Culture in Orléans, France.

SPECULATIONS

12

The tourist negotiates city space by relentlessly collecting images, text, guidebooks, and maps in an attempt to sustain the ongoing delirium of a journey, artificially imparting meaning and relevance to otherwise banal circumstances and occurrences.

Postcards from various places are not only evidence of such engineered pilgrimages but also vehicles for transferring and reviving experience. These collected images offer physical evidence of the intricate matrices of desire and curiosity that prompt the journey to continue.

Today touristic experiences resemble military maneuvers, they are planned in advance to secure the best view, the perfect light, the finest meal, or simply to beat the crowds. The tourist meanders and consumes incessantly, becoming familiar while always remaining a stranger, forming immediate and rarefied nostalgia out of each event and occurrence.

The video camcorder is the weapon of choice for such methodical *dérives*. The images it captures are not only fluid representations of a particular place; they also construct a precise narrative of events in which the salutation "WISH YOU WERE HERE" is replaced by "YOU ARE HERE." This cliché is itself critical, adding significance to an otherwise inconsequential experience.

To participate in the cliché is to be a tourist, an impartial observer of one's own observations.

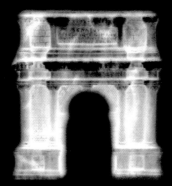

MEDITATIONS

Architecture is not, as some would have it, a reworking of tradition, nor is it a futile interplay of metaphors and poetry used to justify self-expression. Architecture surfaces only after the act of making is brought to completion; that is, once the act of making architecture stops and it remains a residue on some uncharted horizon.

To draw is to deceive, to play a game of control over a nebulous terrain of disparities dominated by the incalculable. Architects must persevere in a fluctuating reality composed of momentary relapses, split-second reasoning, and the absurd logic of the sound bite. Abandoning traditional rules in favor of chance and the unanticipated allows one to move through a landscape of uncertainties, liberated from the incessant desire to create "the new." If all goes well, one emerges having accomplished very little.

Disrupting the linear process invites a convoluted trajectory that is perhaps equally problematic, yet appealing for the delirium it inspires. New architecture might be liberated from the tedium of comprehension and the presumption of knowledge. Dissonant and spontaneous, this architecture would encourage a fluctuating hierarchy of beauty that is removed from the madness of commodification and the superficial. It would invite one to forget the self and instead surrender to amnesia, a forgetfulness. No longer should architects merely seek to provide comfort and embellishment; we should also make provisions for the impending collapse of modernity. This is an architecture liberated from the nostalgia and nausea of the trustworthy, architecture somewhere between cacophony and order.

Cities today are molded by consensus, by an ethic constructed and controlled by media, advertising, and marketing. Today the desire to circumvent stasis and control propels the public to search for constant change and increasing novelty. New forms of architecture emerge not as a result of revising scientific models of certainty but rather through the reconfiguration of simulated realms and of our notions of reality. City space can be deciphered today by illuminating the unattainable and empowering the circumstantial.

This, then, is a dictum: Run among the ghosts and dine with angels.

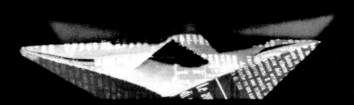

PSEUDO-ARCHITECTURE

"Congratulations ladies and gentlemen, on having invented the greatest time waster in all of history." These words, uttered in an RCA lab in 1934, introduced the invention we now know as television. It was not only an entertainment apparatus but also an instrument for disseminating information, an aperture allowing us to observe the development of communications technology. Decades later, simultaneous live broadcasts from the Golden Gate and Brooklyn bridges entranced the nation and exemplified the media's unprecedented ability to condense space and time.

With the Rodney King arrest in Los Angeles in 1991 television transformed the representation of an isolated event into a widespread icon of disenfranchisement. The ubiquitous video camcorder became an arbiter of meaning and reality as repeated broadcasts of the video footage of King's arrest and beating incited an urban revolt. Once removed from its physical context and meticulously reconstructed in the form of grainy images on tape, the struggle between King and the police transcended subjective reality to emerge as indisputable truth. This spectacle was spatial from inception to outcome: it occurred initially in the real space of a city street, was choreographed into televised space, and ended as a riot that altered vast portions of a cityscape and seized worldwide attention.

In 1993 a telephone conversation in New York was interrupted by an incoming call relaying the news that a bomb had just exploded beneath the twin towers of the World Trade Center. The first caller immediately turned the television to a local news program and observed the catastrophe unfolding in real time. Reporters' descriptions of the blast, smoke, and confusion were embellished with statistics and speculation. From a montage of interviews, file footage, and "expert" opinion the viewer frantically attempted to reconstruct the event with certainty. The World Trade Center bombing symptomized the transformed space of the late twentieth century, in which uncontrolled anticipation creates "pseudo-events" of terrorism. Architecture struggles to remain relevant as a discipline in an age when delirium and fear frequently displace actual events.

A compound housing the Branch Davidian religious sect outside Waco, Texas became the center of national attention in 1993 when inside, a self-proclaimed prophet and his followers refused to follow the laws and customs of American society, preferring to wage a small battle against authorities outside the property's fences. The compound resembled the familiar environment of a suburban community, except that it was surrounded by two "armies." The first consisted of various law enforcement agents from the Bureau of Alchohol, Tobacco and Firearms; the FBI; and local police. The second group, the news media, was stationed some three miles away and armed with long-range microphones and telephoto lenses aimed at the center of the complex. Here, a large rotating satellite dish permitted the individuals sequestered inside to constantly monitor their impending doom. Ten days into the conflict a banner emerged from inside the compound bearing the haunting slogan, "We need help, get the Press."

The current popularity of television programs such as "Eye Witness," "Emergency 911," and "COPS" is evidence that surveillance and voyeurism continue to restructure our image of public space. In these mediated portrayals of real events the city appears as a place devoid of center; as a terrain of confrontation, distortion, and distraction. Further, multimedia and interactive media are creating new forms of occupying, conversing, gathering, and meandering in public that call for new programs for architecture and place-making. The real and tangible meld with the obscure and irreconcilable to forge spaces at once familiar and strange.

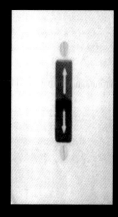

ON RECENT NON-EVENTS

on eventual architecture

Those ignominious machines produce lean (fat-free) buildings.

IMPROVED PLANS FOR IMPOVERISHED SOULS:

Procedure one: All surfaces, including the screen and keyboard, are to be painted, then scraped, as one might dull claws against granite skin. Now, with palette knife in hand, scrawl the face of a goat peering from beyond the viscid monitor. **S T O P**

These are the interminable vapors of convention, the p u r g a t o r y of quality, HYGIENIC ARCHITECTURE FOR THE CIVILIZED. In an age of detachment and indifference, the burlesque show of progress seems to withstand all. Surrounded by this absence of reverie, one finds solace in the caprice of being. The city is again engulfed in a "constructed" plague of which efficiency is but a symptom; the real malady is effect.

Into the viscous black sea that swallowed Venice first fell the fit, and soon after, the docile.

AN ARCHITECTURE OF AMNESIA - ANEMIC ARCHITECTURE:

Procedure two: Tear, then shred the conformist's cloak. Attend to the tarnished kid gloves of progress; they are to be cleaned and polished. Then, along with technology, discard all of it into the gutter!

Marinetti's locomotive has derailed! There will be no more revisions, for revising is an idiot's task. Enigma is only order, and consensus an obscenity. Automobiles will undoubtedly persevere, incising the terrain as deliberately as an executioner.

Procedures (n,n+1):

Crystal and wood that move on invisible rails..Rimbaud
The Precision Weapon..Reverdy
Carefully thrown-back sheets of eggshell...Breton
Doubleply, multigrade, infinitely split-up membrane...Artaud
Knives are signs, and bullets, tears..Éluard
The world is a pill dropped in a glass of water ....J. Vache
The super-rapid position of rest..Duchamp
It has a lead ballast and allows oscillations..Tanguy
The stones are as tormented as flesh; the stones are clouds..Arp
Abandoned vineyards, a tangle of guillotines...Tzara
Objects of different weight, an egg, a glove, and straw...................... ....,,,Roussel
Only useless things are indispensable...Picabia

DEPARTURE 2100hrs; ARRIVAL 0900hrs

The airport signifies neither gate nor portal; rather it is a realm of anticipation based on desire and displacement. Airports make all destinations—whether a neighboring city or a far-off continent—seem equal, their differences inconsequential. What matters in an airport is punctuality, personal identification, and procedure: "Your passport and ticket are in order, thank you . . . Please proceed to gate 32 . . . Your flight is now boarding."

The airport, usually at the city's margin and often well outside its physical limits, is a projection of urban reality. A deafening anonymous din fills the airport's spaces. The waiting areas in all terminals resemble one another despite the passengers' diversity. A plane's fuselage, attached to a departure gate like a prosthesis, becomes an infinitely extruded and nondescript waiting area. Here the traveler's physical mobility is replaced by confinement to a fixed position and prolonged disembodiment.

The video monitors in the aircraft's cabin display information that otherwise remains imperceptible to the passenger: exterior air temperature, ground speed, and the aircraft's current altitude and precise location at any given moment. The flickering computer image of the plane's trajectory appearing on the screens just prior to takeoff lends a feeling of comfort and familiarity by simulating a sense of place in a placeless environment.

A laptop computer is activated once the plane is airborne. A hypertext document flashes on the screen, moving as a dense liquid from one mode to the next, revealing at times an image, a drawing, or text. A keystroke and a click cause the internal fax modem to relay an excerpt of the virtual montage to some specified location thirty thousand feet below. Moments later the computer indicates that an incoming message resides in its random access memory; clicking to another location on the hard drive retrieves the message. The in-flight movie appears on the video screens, bringing all activity in the cabin to a halt as each passenger attaches a headset and surrenders to Hollywood's images of consensus. The flight attendants request that all window shades be lowered; passengers wishing to view the clouds and oceans do so with a sense of guilt and subversion. An attendant peddling duty-free goods and the pilot reporting interesting landmarks below interrupt this otherwise serene, euphoric journey through space and multiple time zones.

The illuminated "Fasten Seat Belt" signs and an abrupt jolt mark the landing. The arrival gates appear to vary only slightly from those designated "departure" at the first airport some four thousand miles away. Postcards, mementos, and other paraphernalia displayed in the airport shops present the only evidence that this place is different from the one left behind. These static representations of distilled events and constructed perfection reveal the strange simulacra of the city: its infrastructure, architecture, and inhabitants.

The air terminal of today is seamlessly linked to all other air-ports (cities) by the archaic means of real time travel. It is a condensed spatial apparatus that substitutes for the city and aspires to be a cybernetic circumstance. To travel today is to experience "urban distillation," a space of distortion.

INTERVIEW 1: CONTEXT

We approach each work as if it is enveloped in context. There is, of course, the physical context, a "field of operations," or set of physical conditions, drawn from the site and/or place to form an operating ground for the architectural project. In Los Angeles, for example, the freeway, the downtown core, the historical district, and the endless horizontality of this particular city compose the physical context. The "phenomenal circumstances" of a place, region, or culture make up another equally important context. The ubiquitous site visit, traditionally entailing physical displacement to an actual place in order to observe its context and conditions, might now mean observing various phenomena related to the site—anything from analyzing a televised spectacle to dissecting an object or deconstructing a text. From this systematic re-reading of the site an implicit re-writing takes place, which of course includes a re-presentation of the given program for a proposed building. As it emerges the architecture itself begins to delineate the third context, "becoming." This allows the work to exist in a state of perpetual transformation that continues after its conception and inevitable completion.

Central to our work is a critique of technology. Architecture is obviously a technological practice in which engineering and manufacturing, for example, are involved from the beginning. But more enigmatic concepts also come into play: communications, surveillance, speed, mutation. This is by no means a novel methodology, only one that, in our view, is seriously neglected in late-twentieth-century architectural discourse and practice.

We are dubious about perceiving architectural production as a sanctimonious act. A process that generates form is not a separate and distinct procedure in architecture. The "poetic" is not a justification for form; this implies using poetry as mere embellishment. Making architecture ultimately is a poetic act, yet one that must be accomplished using structure, light, form, events, and occurrences. Within this framework the body is always a foundation for program, a physical presence used to reconcile experience, movement, and desire.

INTERVIEW 2: ARTIFACTS

While starting a new project recently we hesitated, struck by the emptiness of "beginning," and contemplated the inks, adhesives, pigments, and drawing equipment spread across the work-tables. We thought about the kind of space these archaic implements have always imparted to architecture, and we contemplated the legendary fiction of Brunelleschi confronting the Baptistery doors in Renaissance Florence, lining up tools that were not so different from our own. We began to construct a fictitious architectural history based on various materials—pigments and the decorative tradition . . . plaster and embellishment . . . plastics and modernity—but we quickly realized that the symbolic weight of these materials was due in part to the history of what they have made.

Beneath a pile of discarded photocopies we retrieved a camera, an instrument that has profoundly reconfigured both the conception and outcome of architecture. Were Gustav Eiffel's infinitely static constructions conceived in an attempt to rival the onslaught of photography? Was cinema an inspiration for Antonio Gaudí's curious creations? And did television, with its cathode rays, influence the works of Eero Saarinen and his contemporaries?

During the past century photography and cinema dismantled the contained, predictable status of objects and space. In this century computers and new information technologies undoubtedly have begun to alter our conception of space itself. Even the traditional architecture *atelier* is somewhat obsolete when one considers drawing digitally and sending drawings, images, and text via fiber optic cable.

We are surrounded by provocative new tools and technologies that call into question our tattered anachronistic methodologies, yet the architecture profession today is overwhelmed by nostalgia and adheres to the past, reluctant to embrace a provocative, perplexing, uncertain future.

Architecture will forever be in combat with gravity. This battle cannot yield victory, only countless eloquent casualties.

Imagine cranes that move whole parts of cities. Prototypes of such machines exist: a television news briefing of an important global event and the accompanying words from the sponsor propel us eloquently from one place to another, from the meaningful to the meaningless.

A microchip of infinitesimal dimensions has been invented that undoubtedly will alter the precious commodity of history. Imagine, if you will, a "memory-exchange" where every significant and insignificant bit of historical information could be bartered and traded. Thought would increase in value, as would whim and intuition. The exchange would constantly mutate, producing a history of supply and demand and futures of possibility.

Icarus's trajectory released him from architecture. The labyrinth, the womb in which Daedalus devised those marvelous wings, marked the point of departure from oppressive form and initiated a flight toward light and chance.

Airplanes do not defy gravity but rather have conversations with the wind. We have monitored these discussions on occasion. Often their most interesting subjects deal with fear and despair. The wind usually argues that such feelings drive man into her breast; the wing quickly retorts that it can conquer weakness by minor adjustment.

With her smile the moon has frequently seduced man into disrobing her. The relentless courtship of man and the cosmos proves that man is not bound to earth when Eros sits patiently in the wings. Having performed a jig on the moon's surface, however, humankind is now in need of a new ballroom.

Reconnaissance flights are needed now to monitor not the earth's surface, but rather other reconnaissance flights. Probing the landscape during wartime is of no value, as the collected data remains uncertain despite all measures. It is far more compelling to comprehend the act of comprehending.

Times Square is not only the symbolic center of a remarkable metropolis; it is also a vivid paradigm of late-twentieth-century global urbanism. Here the city of New York is distilled into an urban montage of events and phenomena. *Timesquare* is a cinematic field conforming to and yet distorting the speculative whims of real estate development and the hallucinatory ethics of consumerism, entertainment, and tourism. The cacophony of traffic, information, and desire swells in this place of excess and illusion, achieving a perfect chaos saturated with myths and misaligned realities. New architecture spliced into this territory of extremes can only be a faint appendix to an urbanism comprising live theater, fast food, pornography, first-run Hollywood extravaganzas, pickpockets, street vendors, preachers, and tourists. These and many other vectors circulate endlessly through a city space that constantly mutates within a complex global narrative. Reverberating effects from other urban "epilogues"—London, Hong Kong, Paris, and Tokyo—further distort Timesquare's dimensions.

Perpetual Encounters

Performance artists and circuses compete for attention beneath the spectacular advertisements that obliterate the sky and surrounding buildings. Fleeting video images retrieved from global and local television broadcasts sheath the buildings. The surfaces that confront the public are in constant motion, creating a liquidlike atmosphere of logos, messages, and hype which accentuates each experience or event.

Body Shopping

At the intersection of Broadway and Seventh Avenue an oddly shaped glass and steel cage encases body builders and gymnasts whose narcissism and exhibitionism feed the public's incessant appetite for voyeurism. This once-useless traffic island has been transformed into a veritable display case for the body, an organism that seems otherwise inconsequential within this predominantly electronic space.

TV Free

The new Broadcast Terminal transmits an uninterrupted flow of public access television at the top of each hour. The output includes ad hoc talk shows, self-help discussion groups, amateur video, and the latest episode of the epic "Voyeur Vision." Attached to an exterior wall is a device holding thirty-six video camcorders to be used by pedestrians. The comments or events they record are subjected to random editing within the Terminal, where the tapes are processed for transmission between other broadcasts.

Body Surfing

The all-night dentists, manicurists, barbers, tattoo artists, plastic surgeons, and chiropractors receive customers endlessly, promising to soothe both body and ego. The Vacation Salon boasts instant tanning services, while one of the many Morph Lounges nearby can reconfigure your image any way you desire to accompany e-mail messages you might want to send.

Always in Stock

Made-to-order products ranging from pastries to prosthetics are available through voice-activated sidewalk vending machines that deliver the goods to your home before you return. As orders are placed the machines tabulate the popularity of certain products and forward this information immediately to marketing and census groups. The vending machines also allow customers to comment on proposals ranging from new advertising strategies to prospective architectural, theatrical, and other spatial interventions for Timesquare.

Love Gas

Meetings and rendezvous of all genres are possible at multiple locations. At the Love Connect Hotel some people sit passively in the foyer as sound stalls receive anonymous voice and video messages, while others disappear into Profile Construct Booths. On the mezzanine people circulate about holographic projections of various body parts, configuring ideal mates. Some individuals disappear into long narrow hallways where both sexes make random encounters. From here, dimly lit staircases lead to private rooms bisected by large latex walls. These Safe Spots are fitted with personal volume controls that regulate the sound omissions flowing back into the meeting hallways.

Souvenirs

The Souvenir Theaters are always inundated with tourists searching for mementos of their visit to Timesquare. Among the many items available are sample sound recordings of the space at different times of the day, video clips of angles not otherwise obtainable, and a vast assortment of miniature reenactments of events that transpired prior to each tourist's particular visit. A large structure known as Souvenir Tower makes a perfect backdrop for photographing and taping one's visit. The Tower's facades change constantly due to a curtain wall of sound-sensitive materials, ensuring that no two recorded experiences are identical.

Aktion

New films are screened almost nightly and in some cases the actual lots utilized for film production are transported to Timesquare for the opening night festivities. Smaller outdoor cinemas and theaters at every corner show a continuous array of repertoire films or lesser-known theatrical productions. In some cases the rehearsal rooms for these street theaters are visible to passersby, many of whom stop to videotape the dialogues and scenes.

Tableaux Settings

Restaurants and cafés in this area boast perfect views of Souvenir Tower, and those without actual views receive its image via live video feed. The street cafés are constantly busy, and some even have rotating platforms that ensure each patron a moment of outdoor seating. In the more expensive establishments waiters and waitresses are equipped with inconspicuous recording and translating devices that allow them to record and retrieve orders in any language or dialect.

Nacht Musik

The Vox-Box is another popular gathering place in Timesquare. Here clients rent private glass rooms overlooking a vast open space that could be either a dance floor or a large group *karaoke* theater. Special meeting spaces, bars, cafés, and Refresh Zones line a circular trough around the perimeter of the open space. Lobbies have several Identity Exchange Rooms used frequently by people arriving straight from work or travel.

No Exit

A number of smaller, more intimate bars and lounges are also located throughout Timesquare. The most popular of these is the Limited-Time Café attached to the exterior of Souvenir Tower. The café travels up and down the entire forty stories of the Tower, providing dramatic views of the action below. Patrons check into the bar on the ground floor and occupy it for precisely one hour, the duration of a full trip up the Tower and back down again.

Re-lapses

The quieter locations for rendezvous are in the Silence Lounges concealed in various locales around Timesquare. Two such Lounges, The Cage and The Burrows, are hidden in back alleys. The Cage is a small, dimly lit space that encourages patrons to bring their own recordings, which are played on individual table-mounted players connected to pairs of headsets. The Burrows is beneath Timesquare and descends more than thirty meters into the earth. The spiral floor has various seating areas that overlook a gaping void from which the sounds of under- ground traffic and trains intermittently escape.

Critical Path

Public artworks are everywhere in Timesquare, especially at a space called the Zoo-Trop. Here in this cubic volume artworks of diverse scales and genres are constantly arranged, rearranged, and ultimately discarded throughout the day. The Zoo-Trop's immense interior often overwhelms visitors, who can ride one of the many escalators to view the latest works at closer proximity or from various vantage points. A large liquid crystal screen above the entrance outside displays descriptions of the exhibited works, various critical reviews, and the corporate sponsor's logo.

INTERVALS

A steel trestle bridge spanning a gorge 180 feet deep and one-third of a mile across was the center of media attention after a strange sighting there was reported. Although the turn-of-the-century bridge traversed an area thought to be largely uninhabitable, a curious tourist surveying the area witnessed someone climbing up the structure from the valley below. Later investigations revealed that in fact someone had been living in a ramshackle structure attached to the underside of the bridge. This domicile was constructed of found objects and materials: old doors and window frames, metal from car chassis and fenders, and other discarded building materials. The well-camouflaged structure was tethered to the weblike bridge with rope and electrical cable.

The odd house was dismantled immediately after its discovery, and its various parts returned to their probable place of origin—the local dump. Discarded along with these materials was a collection of household objects that had been powered by electrical cables attached to power lines traveling along the roadway above: kitchen appliances, a ham radio, a television, and a telephone. A large collection of carefully compiled, indexed, and stored newspaper and magazine clippings afforded other indications of this individual's personality and preoccupations.

"The Spiderman," as he became known in local press reports, never surfaced again at this particular location, although sightings at other bridges nearby were reported in the months that followed.

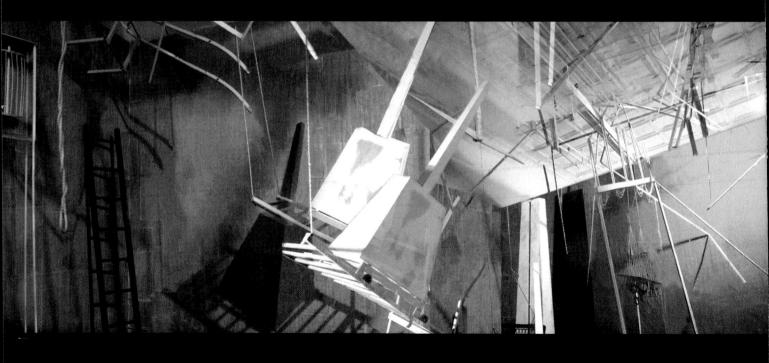

The ancient technique of collage has long been used to scrutinize visuality, perception, and comprehension. In this century alone, painting, literature, poetry, film (montage), architecture, and other arts have accelerated the development of this technique through their sometimes arbitrary juxtaposition of disparate and dislocated elements. With the advent of digital technologies such assemblies have crossed new thresholds of representation and information manipulation.

The history of the image formed the basis for the Optigraph studies. Perspective, framing, ordering, composition, and processes long-associated with optic experiences were scrutinized by way of these experiments. The studies afford untold opportunities for combining, splicing, fusing, merging, and reassociating artifacts and spatialities; they constitute a representational method of describing and inscribing space which calls into question our timeworn visual practices.

The Optigraphs began as "surveillances" of found images extracted from newspapers, magazines, travel brochures, technical manuals, entertainment guides, television advertising, and any other medium offering evidence of the cult of the image. This processing, recording, and playback, combined with phenomenological vectors such as noise, distraction, anonymity, delirium, and hallucination, yielded architectures that peered precariously beneath the last vestiges of modernity, revealing concealed territories of enigma, strangeness, and delusion.

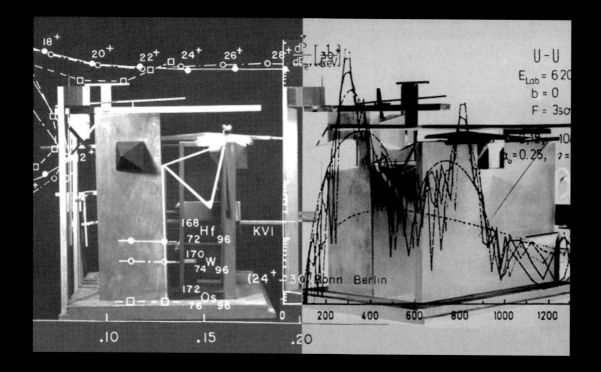

1. Standing or situated in front of; facing. *The house across the way is directly opposite this one.*

3. In logic, differing in quantity or quality, or in both as propositions or theses.

5. The act of opposing; an attempt to check, restrain, or defeat resistance.

9. In rhetoric, a figure that joins two things which seem incompatible.

The kings have only one vacant square between them.
Fight, attack, oppose, resist.

Cri·te·ri·a [Gk *opsis*, sight, appearance, vision; and *metron*, measure]

1 a : to choose   **b :** to wish for   **c :** to desire
2 : by desire
3 : expressing desire or wish
4 : an organ of sight; an eye

(a) The angle between two lines drawn from the two extremities of an object to the center of a lens and tending to meet at some distance in front of the eyes.

(b) An instrument used in surveying, for laying out lines at right angles to each other. It consists of a circular brass box containing an index and horizon glasses, fixed at an angle of forty-five degrees.

Op·ti·graph [Gk *optikos*, in other senses, and *graphein*, to write]

1 : a telescope made for the purpose of copying landscapes
2 : an instrument for producing pictures on a screen
3 : an instrument for measuring the limits of vision and determining imperfection
4 : the measure of the mind's capacity for or interest in what has already occupied it

(a) A polished surface of metal or any other material suitable for reflecting rays of light, which are converted into a cone upon entering the lens and issued as a hollow cylinder.

(b) The consequent production of two distinct images in which terrestrial objects appear to be farther from the horizon than they are in reality.

(c) An optical instrument for viewing distant objects and terrain. It assists the architect in two ways: first, by enlarging the visual angle at which a distant object is seen, thereby manipulating the object's scale; second, by collecting and conveying to the eye a broader scope of possibilities.

These interrogations of Berlin's undercarriage are "readouts" extracted from the Optigraph mechanism as it retrieved a hypothetical architecture latent beneath the Berlin Wall. They are preparatory charts for *eventual* structures inspired by and evocative of the perplexing marks left on the Wall by those who escaped, perished, and yearned by it. This work was analogous to performing an autopsy or detecting a computer virus concealed in some arcane circuitry.

Excerpts from "OPTIGRAPH 3: Berlin Readouts, Miniseries 3"
Originally published in its entirety by Columbia University Graduate School of Architecture, Planning and Preservation, 1990

A machine stands mute beneath the rubble of the now-defunct Wall. Perhaps the machine was once useful in surveying the **FRONTIER.** Architecture, too, is suspended here in this trench, mutilated and beheaded. All around are monoliths, displaced and ridiculous, immersed in a sea of concrete and steel. The mechanism's precise instruments are useless underneath such dense and imposing shrapnel.

Two spheres of equal dimension, traveling toward each other at unknown speed, appear on the screen. These converging trajectories may never terminate; however, the mere possibility generates a multiplicity of events. Readings of the ever-decreasing distance between the two bodies generate infinite number sequences and orbits. The initial registrations of these combatants on a thin plate are but a scrawl, yet their emergence signifies becoming.

The unremitting commotion of the printer mimics all emblems of order.

Beneath this wall an OPTIC city perseveres, and the tools and weapons of perfection are scattered throughout these strange depths, bathed in the dim light of knowledge. The monitor reveals a spherical surface, increments of curvilinear terrain beneath two undulating lines. A new field emerges and is enlarged by the manipulation of certain lenses.

The wave particles plummet through minuscule diaphragms and apertures, only to expire while suspended in the abyss. Other curious instruments for measure and calculation relentlessly inscribe the entire volume. A residue, or "ghosting effect," is the only evidence of these inscriptions, and the eroding metals and glass casings transport trace elements of inexplicable origin. Some of the particles that fill the far reaches are complex and unstable, although a minor adjustment briefly stabilizes them. Gears and cogs drive other, more delicate mechanisms high above mirages and shadows of archaic machinery. These elusive simulations perpetually dissect the appearing figures, while the Optigraph's own dimension is now completely immeasurable. You are no longer capable of piloting this machine; the space it spawned is no longer tangible.

The object has been eradicated.

Optigraph 3: Berlin Readout *operation a*

Optigraph 3: Berlin Readout *operations b-c*

Optigraph 3: Berlin Readout *operations d-e*

In Paris in 1848 craftsmen and artisans revolted by erecting a magnificent barricade that barred the west entrance to Faubourg Saint-Antoine. This three-story-high, seven-hundred-foot-long construction spanned the streets, with nineteen smaller barricades branching from it.

"It was made of paving stones, scrap iron, rubble, floorboards, bundles of old rags, cabbage stalks, broken chairs, up-ended carts, It was big, and it was small . . . . It was the sweepings of a whole people, a lumberyard of bronze and wood and iron and stone, and you would have thought that one huge broom had swept it into place . . . . Senseless it was, but heroic too."

Victor Hugo

Surveillance 001:

On a number of occasions the Optigraph mechanism was placed before the Pont Neuf, in the Place Dauphine. Each passing moment there was recorded, then collapsed onto the previous moment until a final inscription resulted. The Optigraph produced an extensive list of events for this site overlooking the Seine, all interwoven into the recorded images of a fairground, a bazaar, an employment exchange, bookstalls, a card factory, a dairy, and various *cabinets d'aisance inodores.*

At the Place Dauphine one could have a tooth pulled, watch a tightrope dancer, buy a Fragonard painting, pick up a new book or first edition, arrange to go up in a balloon, take fencing lessons, or observe a surgical demonstration.

Surveillance 002:

The Optigraph took a number of other readings along the boulevard du Palais and rue de la Cité. Eventually the Optigraph was set before the Hôtel Dieu at twenty-one degrees north of Nôtre Dame. The Optigraph recorded architecture that contrasted with the present buildings in this zone surrounding the cathedral. In lieu of judicial and administrative facilities, there appeared a collection of "aromatic" dens and places for producing every type of furniture imaginable at the highest possible standard: a "Duchesse" for relaxation, a "Voyeuse" for watching, a "Chauffeuse" to facilitate undressing, a "Chaise en Confessionel," a "Confidante," and a "Tête a Tête." In this manufacturing quarter craftsmen and artists might transform wood, bronze, velvet, tin, cotton, paper, and china into beautiful and enigmatic utilitarian objects.

Surveillance 003:

From another stationary point, this time in the Palais de Justice, the Optigraph probed a precinct of enlightened curiosity—the environs surrounding Sainte Chapelle. Here one may watch private theatrical performances or the frequent arrival and departure of various airborne machines. In this place is an exemplary manufacturer of fine velvet, a refuge for dilettante artists, and the Museum of Automata, with its vast and impressive collection of machines. Among the items on display are figures that play the flute, beat drums, and carry on games of chess. One may also see an automatic duck that quacks and flaps its wings, and an automatic artisan that can produce an endless chain of links.

Hyperfine Splitting addresses the impact of the computer on all aspects of human activity. In this series we used digital photography, scanning, video animation, drawing, and modeling to capture architectural moments in an otherwise continuous, fluid action of making space. These works appear here as glimpses into a world we are only beginning to experience as text-based; for example, through e-mail, MUD's, MOO's and other interactive interfaces.

Thus far the typical use of digital technology in architecture has been limited to enhancing efficiency, productivity, and the visual impact of the work. Computers have been deployed primarily to emulate traditional modes of production; to replicate ink drafting, simulate perspectival views and the experience of walking through a building, and improve the means by which alterations and changes are made. As a result of this technology, however, new models of spatiality are emerging that no longer conform to anachronistic notions of space as finite and static.

In a mirror in which all is inverted, space congeals into a liquid not unlike mercury. With the appropriate gear one may pass through mirrors and swim in the dense interior. Orpheus fell through such an aperture to rescue Eurydice from death. In this zone there is no dimension or direction, only light that provides propulsion.

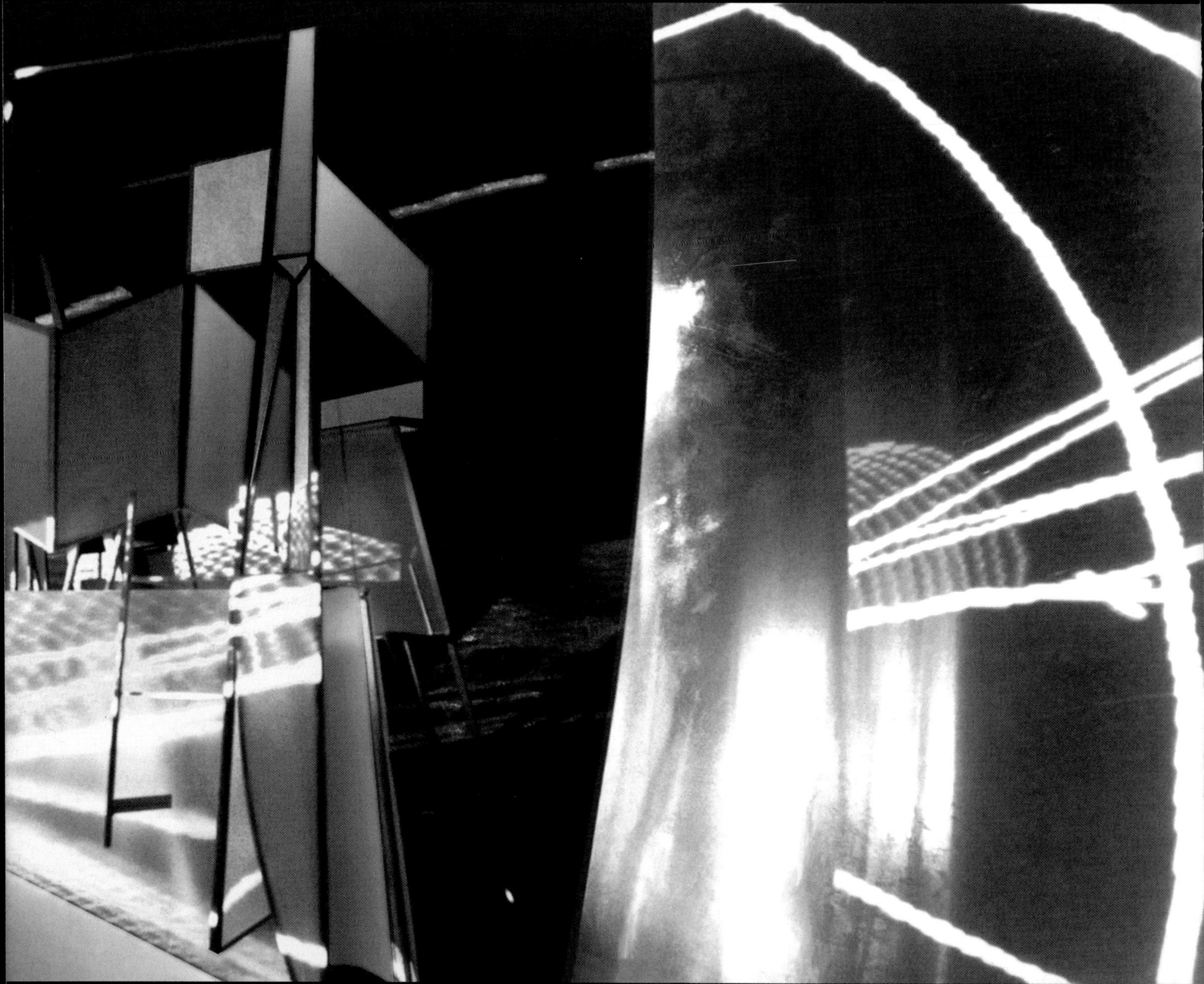

Hyperfine Splitting 006 *Surveillance sequence b*

From a single catastrophic moment a space emerges, made only of light. The space changes relentlessly and is without form or structure. Then, in an instant, a vast array of elements is revealed, each one folding upon the other, reconfiguring limitless possibilities. We are now at the threshold of an uncharted landscape, well beyond the sanctuary of order and reason. Here, concealed beyond places inviting yearning and anticipation, we discover an architecture that perseveres.

PROJECTS

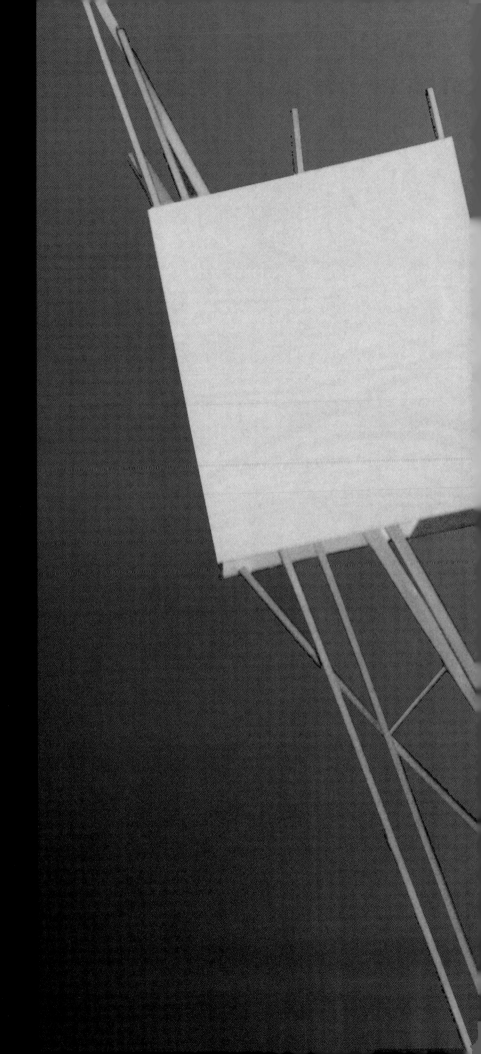

The city of Lanciano on the Adriatic coast in central Italy held an open international competition for architects and city planners, with two main objectives: to establish a long-term development strategy for appropriate growth in future decades, and to solicit building proposals that embraced the city's rich history and urban morphology, which is a hybrid of medieval accretion and modern rational planning.

The scheme developed from an interest in the schism between urban growth and historical preservation. Currently Lanciano is sited around a river valley that severs the city's medieval quarter from its encroaching nineteenth-century grid. The river once carried runoff from nearby mountains to the Adriatic sea and was subsequently deviated underground. Today it is a chasm between the old city—predominantly a tourist attraction—and the nineteenth-century development, where most of the local population lives. This scheme attempts to reconcile the disparate parts of the modern town of Lanciano and determine the elements necessary for its future growth.

Initially the paintings of Italian Futurists Carlo Carra and Gino Severini were used as literal grounds for exploring possible interventions in Lanciano. The early-twentieth-century avant-garde in Italy anticipated the schism between modernity and tradition and, through the poetics of speed and movement, sought to reveal a world reconciled through difference. Their visions incorporated and utilized the machine paradigm and the dynamism of urban life. With the vigor of the new century upon them, the Futurists used graphic, sculptural, and textual references to make paradoxical the staid, highly embellished history of nineteenth-century Italy. This urban proposal overlays and juxtaposes lines and volumes in the valley of Lanciano in figures reminiscent of the Futurists' geometries. These traces and manipulations yielded an abstracted landscape from which a certain urbanism and, more specifically, a certain architecture could materialize.

The program, on the other hand, reflects quite different concerns. Based on the understanding that Lanciano's urbanism simultaneously embraces and resists modernity, new buildings and spaces were designed to work with the city's inherent dichotomy and its struggle with its own complex history. The programs for these spaces derived from the encyclopedic tradition, a means of scientifically classifying and organizing the world. Our intention was to accumulate an endless selection of functions and programs that would propel the town into the next century as an urban prototype predicated on disparity, action, and event.

The scheme consists of housing flanking an immense botanical garden, an opera house and theater sited above an existing Roman bath, historical and military museums, a dairy farm, and a church suspended over an artificial river. The five-hundred-meter-long aqueduct spans the entire site, carrying water to not only the new development (organized alongside the aqueduct), but also the city's medieval quarter and beyond to irrigate the adjoining valleys. Under this suspended river are public baths, water mills, and promenades. At its terminus huge aviaries containing great varieties of birds lift the steel frame structure of the aqueduct high above the valley floor. In the town's main piazza a 360-degree screen displaying information and entertainment bathes an old square in flickering video light. A second elevated bridge containing merchants' housing and a collection of specialized stores cuts across the site diagonally, connecting the old city center with a new industrial zone for artisanal production.

The Lanciano urban design proposal was submitted to the jury as a five-hundred-year plan that not only solves immediate infill and occupancy problems but might also offer a prototype for other towns struggling to reconcile history, modernity, tourism, nostalgia, and relevance.

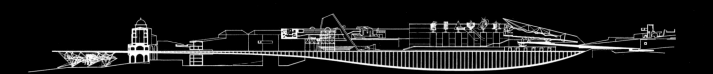

Lanciano Urban Plan

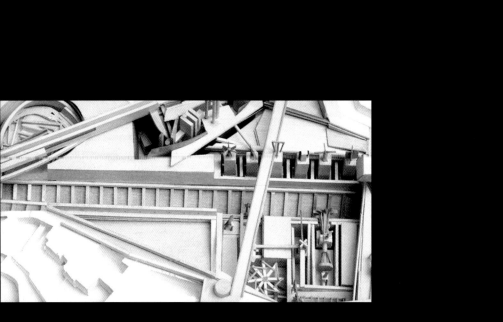

LOS ANGELES WEST COAST GATEWAY: THE STEEL CLOUD

In 1987 New York City celebrated the centennial of the Statue of Liberty; in 1988 the mayor of Los Angeles launched an international competition for the West Coast Gateway, a monument to immigration from the Pacific Rim.

For the ancient Greeks and Egyptians monuments married symbolic imagery with technology, a tradition that continued until the late nineteenth century. The Statue of Liberty standing watch over New York's harbor was one of the culminating works in this trajectory. Today the Statue of Liberty symbolizes not only individual freedom and collective memory but also the very city whose inlet it occupies.

The Eiffel Tower constructed for the Paris International Exposition of 1889 was a symbol of the modern age. Parisians ridiculed it as vulgar and arrogant and proposed a number of schemes for its removal, while the press went to great lengths to discredit its architect and engineer, Gustav Eiffel. Today the Tower stands as a national icon, permanently entrenched in the psyche and geography of present-day Paris. Roland Barthes's reflections on the Tower's "totally useless" nature and "infinitely useful" presence were no doubt influenced by Eiffel's claim that the building was only really useful in its role as the tallest structure ever built.

Tatlin's *Model for a Monument to the Third International,* completed in 1920 and exhibited at the Eighth Pan-Russian Moscow Congress of Soviets, represented a project even more technologically ambitious than Eiffel's tower. Tatlin's web of steel was to be larger in scale and magnitude than its Paris counterpart, and was occupied by three immense kinetic chambers. Each of these rotated at a different rate: once per day, once per month, and once per year. Political propaganda was the essential motive for this work, but the arrival of radio and telecommunications technology also prompted this convoluted structure, a symbol of the utopian aspirations of the machine age.

Today we view technology with awe and reticence. Attempting to place the monument in the context of the late twentieth century, therefore, we proposed a project inspired by optical phenomena, surveillance and telecommunications technology, computer simulation, and the inspired and problematic proliferation of information.

This monument is located directly above the median strip of the Hollywood Freeway in Los Angeles, where automobiles offer freedom from an urban landscape often perceived as hostile and alienating. Here is a city where privacy and evasion, glamour and fantasy contrast with the anticipation of disaster and the fear of rupture and breakdown at many levels. The Steel Cloud is a prop that attempts to mend this bifurcated city. Embodying Marcel Duchamp's axiom that modernity is "the super-rapid position of rest," this architectural assemblage makes scale and meaning purposely disconcerting. Aquariums and suspended landscapes hover above the skyline and oscillate to its hidden rhythms. The lifted horizon lines that delineate this structure meld with the endless horizontality that is Los Angeles. Here galleries, libraries, theaters, cinemas, parks, and plazas all intersect the fluid and transient space of the city. The Steel Cloud is architecture for the post-information age, devoid of perspective, depth, frames, or enclosure; it is a prop for a place where hallucination and fiction temper vivid reality.

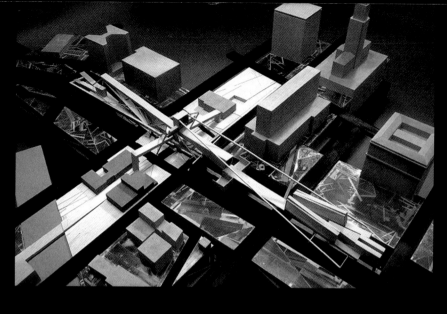

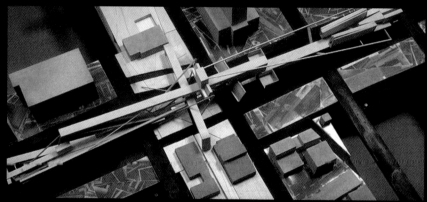

Los Angeles West Coast Gateway: The Steel Cloud

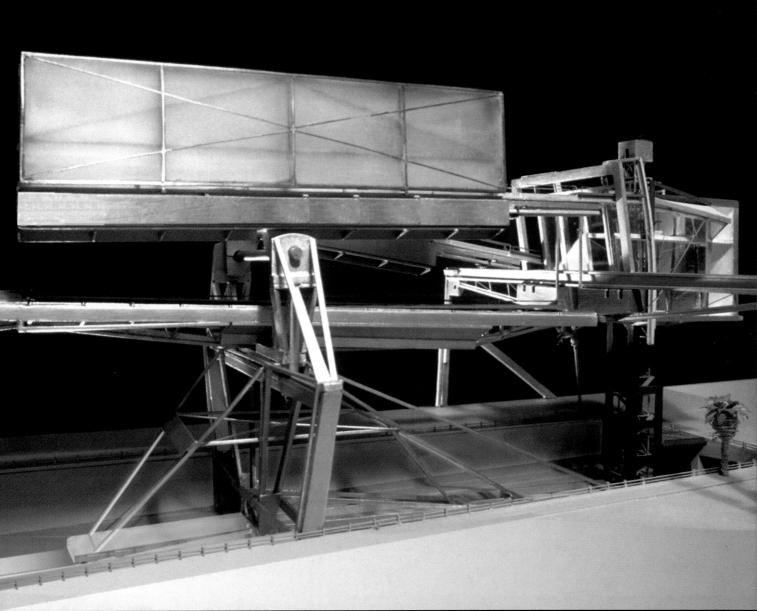

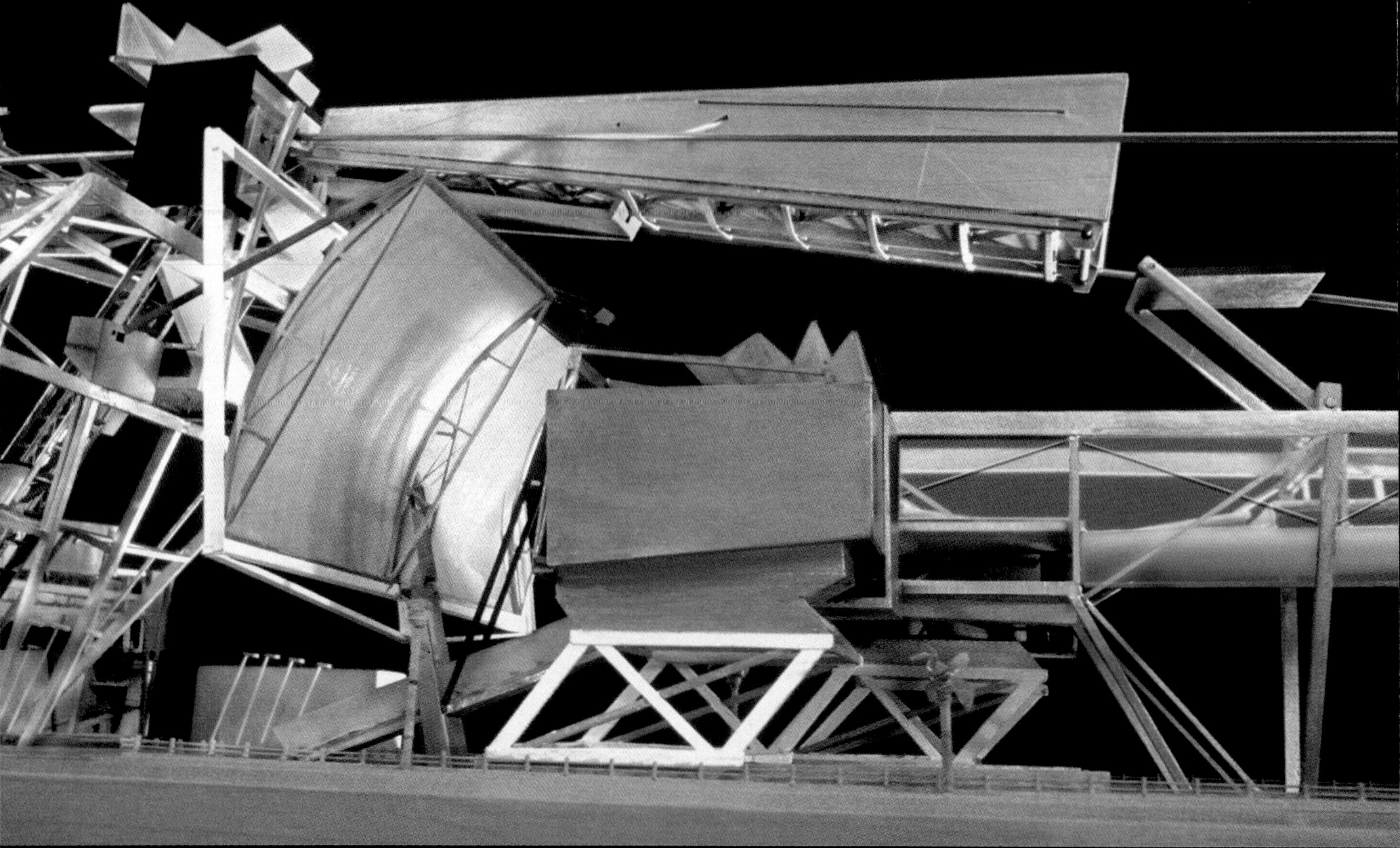

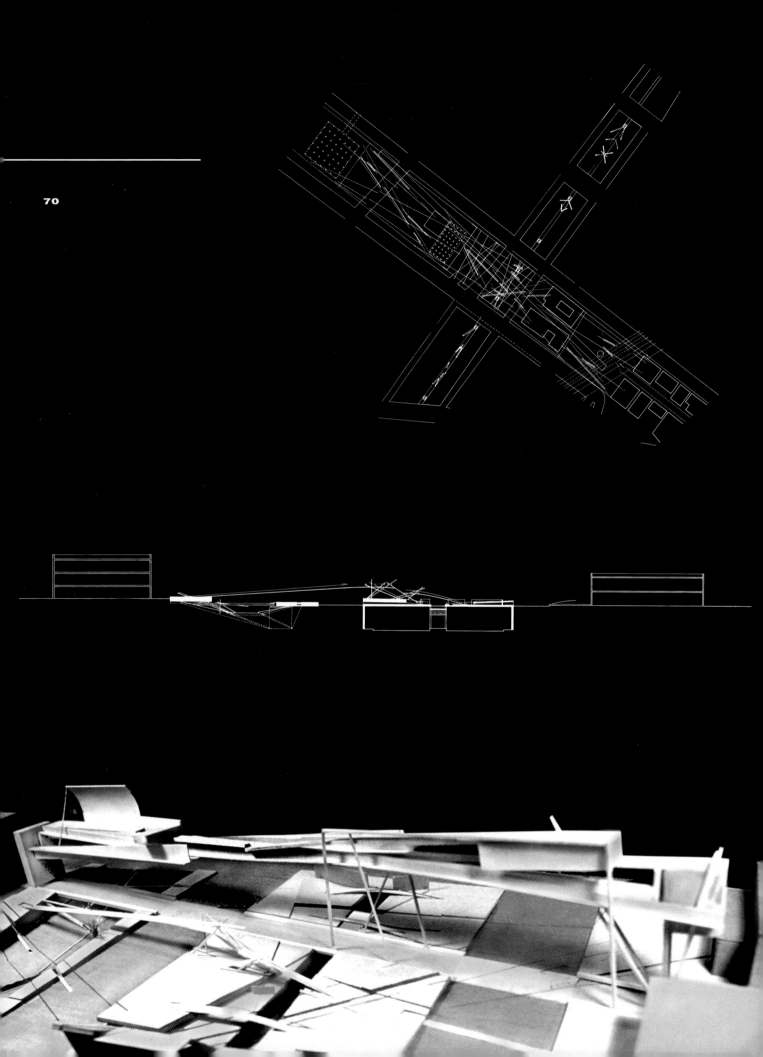

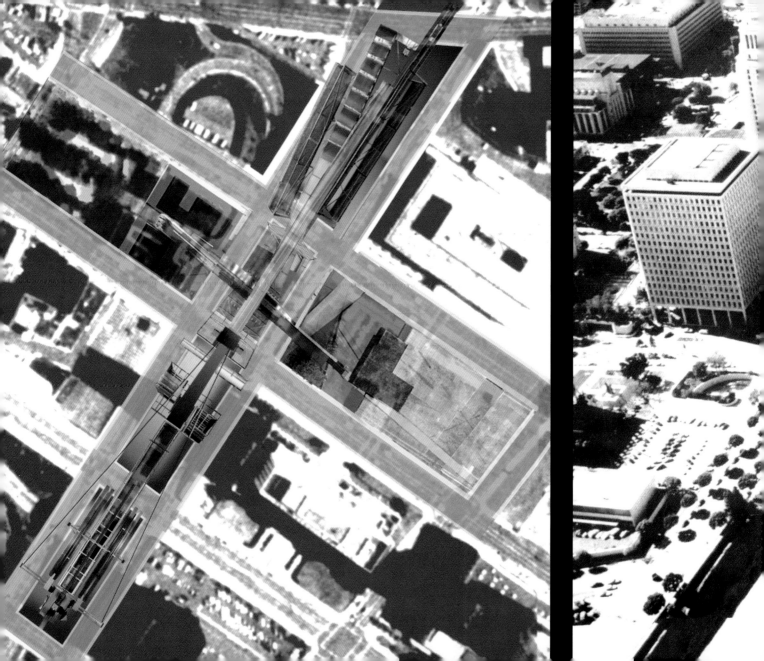

Los Angeles West Coast Gateway: The Steel Cloud

The government of Egypt, in conjunction with UNESCO, sponsored a design competition for a new library in Alexandria recalling the great ancient library that occupied a similar site along the Mediterranean shore two thousand years ago. Today the rich history of this place is overshadowed by political strife and calamity; an architecture based on myth and nostalgia or synthetic histories would only avoid confronting the harsh realities of this paradoxical land. From this architecture the new library struggles to surface, not merely as a facility for learning but as a transcription of past and present.

At the height of its power in the third century B.C., Alexandria was a center for Hellenistic and Jewish culture, and the largest city in the Mediterranean. Ships docked at the port were often detained until all the texts on board were meticulously transcribed and the facsimiles stored in the library's enormous vaults. This relentless desire to acquire knowledge and amass information resulted in the creation of the most extensive collection of texts of that time, until a fire tragically reduced the great library to ashes. According to popular legend, the only text to survive was a treatise on alchemy; its coveted contents were passed down through generations and contributed to our present knowledge of algebra, chemistry, geology, cartography, physics, and medicine.

The main component of the new library acknowledges this mythopoetic history and Egypt's cultural aspirations today. It consists of an uninterrupted hall, 350 meters long and seven stories high, that rises gradually from the eastern part of the site toward the Mediterranean Sea. This enormous alabaster-clad volume stores the immense collection of texts. Here exterior light filters through massive walls, bathing the interior volume in amber light. Automated trolleylike vehicles travel back and forth across the entire length of the space, mechanically retrieving documents from the towering stacks and delivering them to the public reading rooms high above. Glass bridges suspended twenty meters above the floor of this vault of text afford spectacular views of the entire collection and offer a dramatic transition between the cacophonous city and the library's contemplative interior.

These glass passageways lead to an outdoor court above the fluctuating ground of the sculpture garden. To one side, beyond an inclined wall sheathed in cascading water, are the Ptolemy Hall, Calligraphy Museum, Science Museum, and Observatory. Opposite is the main entrance leading to a labyrinthine collection of reading rooms, computer workstations, study carrels, and a large public reading hall directly above the vault of text. At the end of this hall, set against views of the Mediterranean, an immense glass prism encloses towering book stacks that emerge from the space below. Beyond this hall are housed rare book collections, the most sacrosanct rooms in the library. These spaces occupy the niches and folds in an enormous wall that faces the sculpture garden. A collage of texts is inscribed into the wall's inclined surfaces; at times the text pierces through the surfaces, allowing light to filter into the somber interior. From the garden these etched planes appear as an enormous eroding book set against the limitless horizon beyond.

An inclined plane cuts through the entire site from east to west, linking the city with the Mediterranean and, more important, symbolically merging Egypt with the horizon. Viewed from either the surrounding urban area or the sea, the library appears to simultaneously rise from and sink into a shifting terrain of stone. These partially embedded forms recall the ambiguous scale of ancient Egypt's monuments and tombs, submerged in a sea of sand, as Napoleon's troops might once have come upon them. Viewed from the sea, the library seems to be a mirage on the horizon, where at one moment the shape of a ship's prow appears, and at another, the form of an obelisk caught in a continuous state of dissolution. This is a place that alludes to a forgotten past and a culture that today is steeped in uncertainty. Here within the crevices and folds one finds retreat and solitude; it is in the shadows that this architecture congeals. The new Alexandria Library is without hierarchy or center; it emerges as a vital place for sustaining memory and enriching minds amid the struggle for identity and the yearning for place.

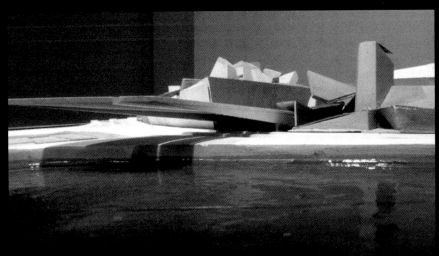

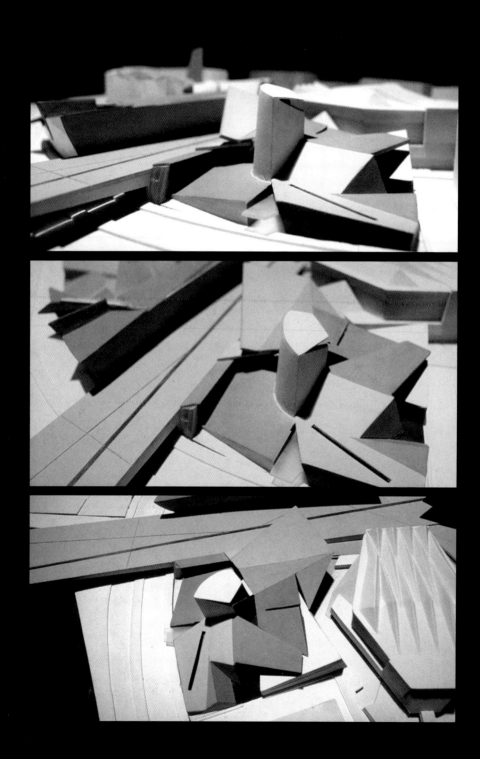

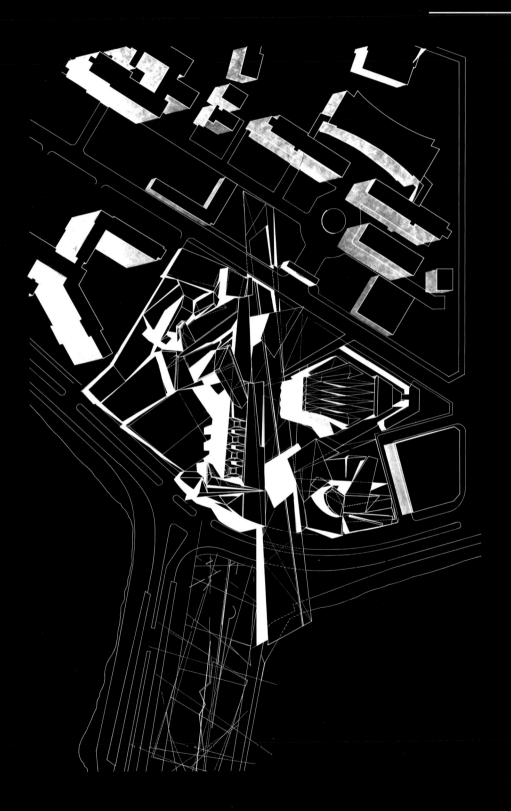

Alexandria Library

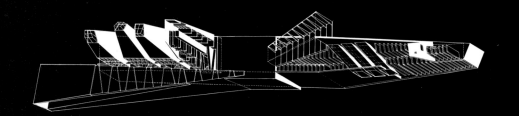

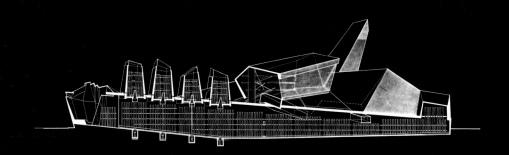

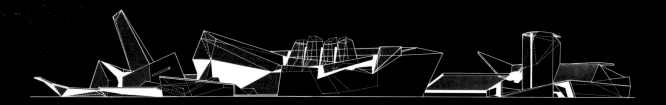

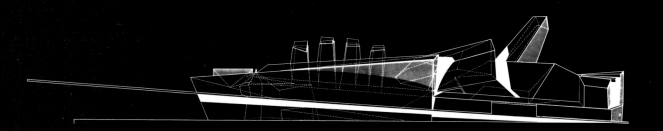

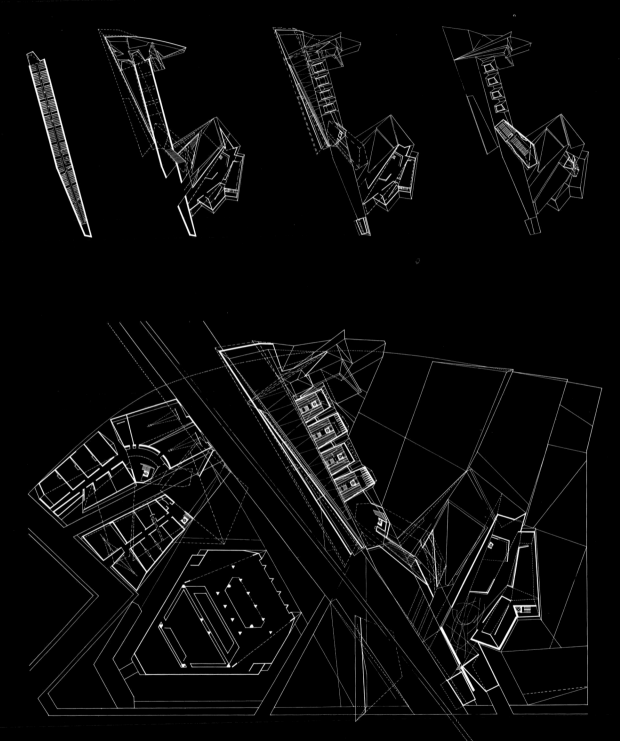

Alexandria Library

A survey of maps, tourist guides, and other by-products of tourism, espionage, and marketing provided a glimpse into the perplexing reality of the former USSR. Central Intelligence Agency maps represented a city quite distinct from the one in KGB documents or the American Express tourist guidebook. Each of these maps depicted yet another rendition of the same city; together they revealed a context of constantly fluctuating dimensions steeped in dissonant resonances.

The Moscow State Theater project includes conventional chamber theaters, experimental performance spaces, and a hotel for traveling theater troupes, all set within the pristine environment of a seventeenth-century garden. The new buildings stand in sharp contrast to the existing neoclassical structures within this walled enclave. The scheme evolved along certain lines and traces of resistance to uncover an architecture that defies the staid character of the classical gardens and surroundings and offers instead a vital place of overt disclosure.

The program challenged the apparent schism between public performance and private production, deliberately obscuring spatial borders to expose the hidden territory between spectator and spectacle. A linear fly tower links the various theaters and set shops while carrying props and backdrops above the gardens and across the Moscow skyline. These strange elements hover high above the urban landscape and create curious juxtapositions that implicate even the city in the unfolding of theatrical events.

From within the garden one can look through various apertures into spaces located below grade to observe activity in the set shops, on various sound stages, in rehearsal rooms, and in other areas normally concealed from public view. Over a continuous period of time one could follow the progress—or disjointed development—of a theatrical production, while possibly never attending the actual performance. Spectacles appear elsewhere in the form of kinetic structures such as the traditional chamber theater, where walls retract and banks of seats disengage from their housing for outdoor performances. Once again, architectural program and surrounding context overlap, each calling the other into question. Here theatrical production and day-to-day routine meld together to form a space of interference and distortion.

This is an architecture that resists the historically autocratic context of Soviet society, perhaps offering an appropriate alternative for a public long-preoccupied with disclosure and truth. Here the two distinct but parallel worlds collide. The Moscow State Theater is ultimately a disfigured architecture, unhinged and precarious, inserted into the cityscape of Moscow as an aperture into the next century.

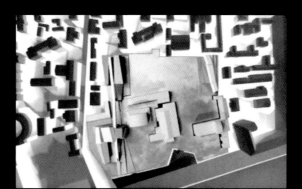

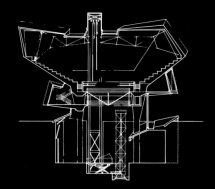

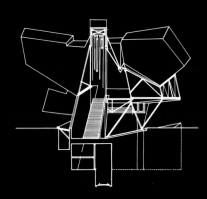

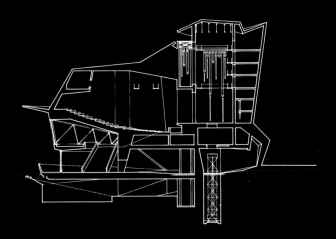

Moscow State Theater

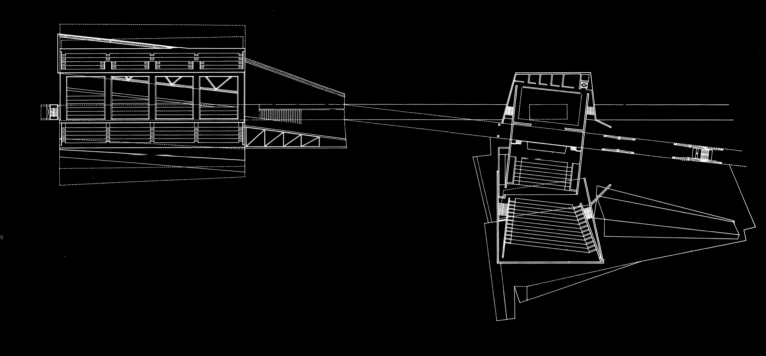
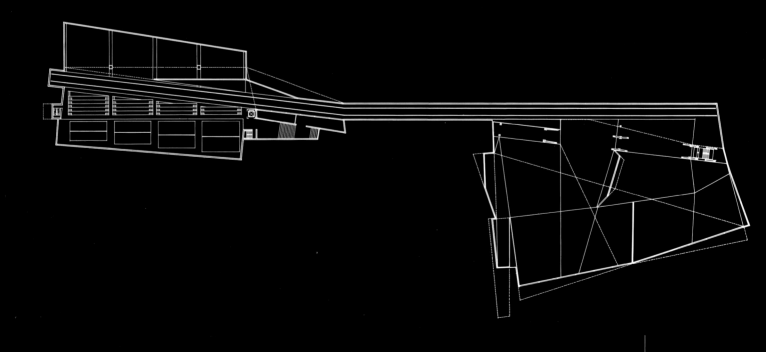

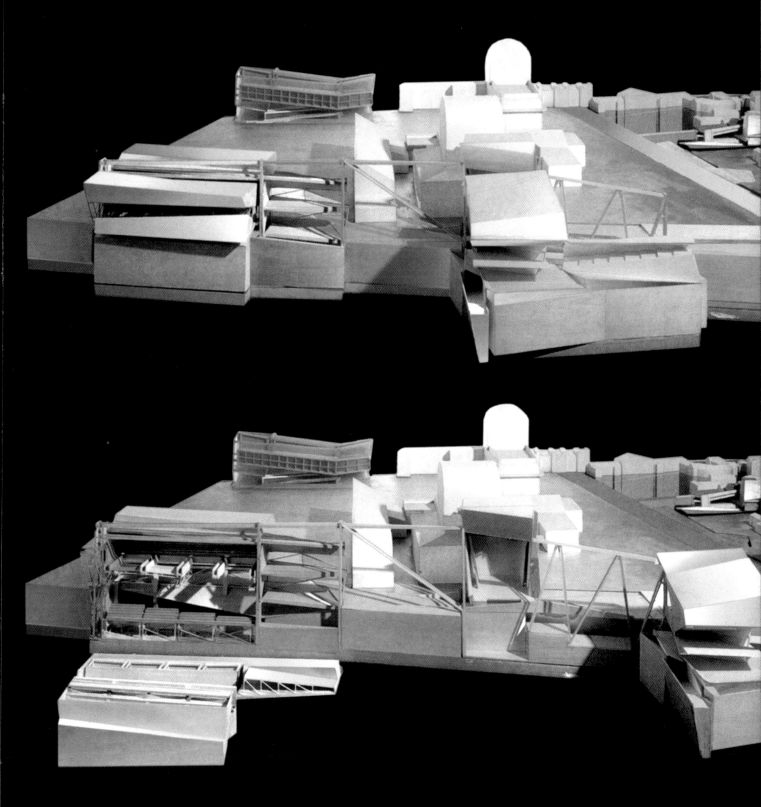

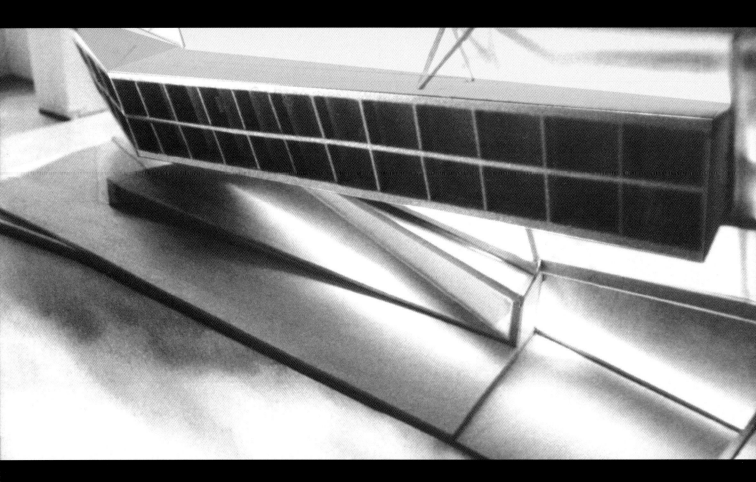

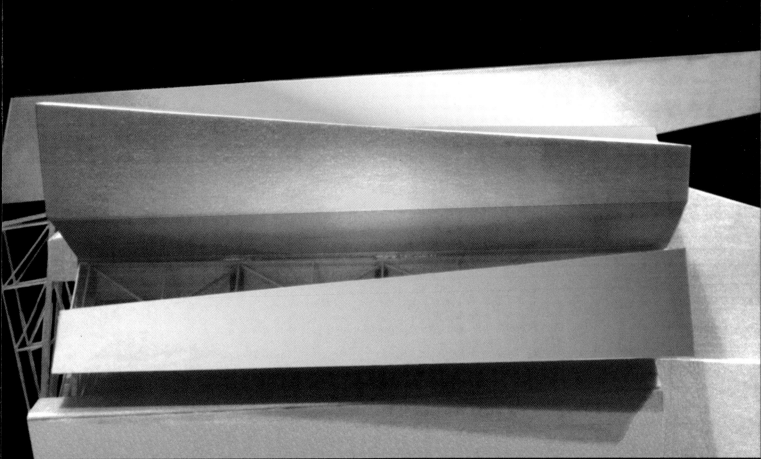

Swiss building code mandates that a nuclear shelter be built with every new home. This obsession with survival was of particular interest, especially when contrasted with the client's somewhat more market-driven requisite that the housings units constitute exclusive residences for skiers and other patrons of Alpine recreational facilities. All six pairs of prospective occupants were childless, youthful, athletic couples targeted by the project's main financier. These people, by virtue of their demographics, were to be provided with breathtaking views, absolute privacy, and immediate access to the auto route to facilitate their return home after weekends of skiing and diversion. These peculiar but actual parameters prompted the project to be conceived as a site for "leisurely escape and escaping leisure."

In response to these concerns, the six dwellings were initially conceptualized as bunkers incising their way into the site, a steep, rocky hillside with dramatic views of the Matterhorn and Swiss Alps. These units received their formal cue from the glacial movement in the surrounding mountains. Here slippage is slow and always unidirectional, a ceaseless grinding and scraping through land masses, unimpeded by obstacles or terrain. These actions of gouging and deflecting, particularly evident in the striated rock, formed the basis for the inscribing process that yielded this architecture. Large expanses of glass set into deformed planes of smooth white concrete became a counterpart to the geological struggle of stone and ice.

While this striation influenced the overall articulation of the dwellings, the cross sections reveal two disparate conditions. On one hand, the retaining wall at the rear of each unit inclines into the steep slope of the hill and away from the unit, allowing daylight to filter deep into its interior. On the other hand, the underground bomb shelter is an antithetical space which, despite its lack of light and air, is traditionally used as a bar and guest room.

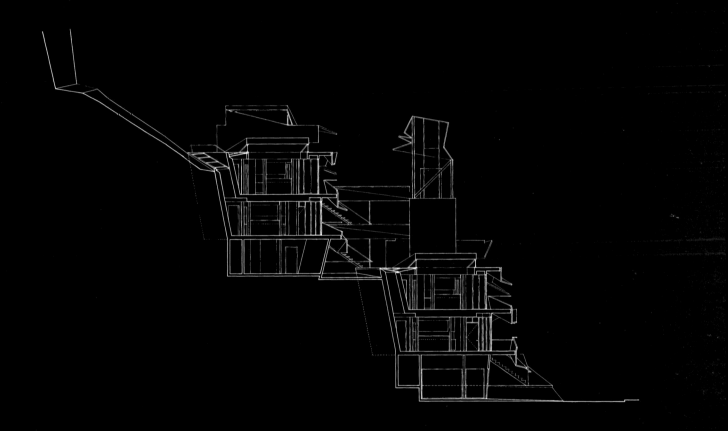

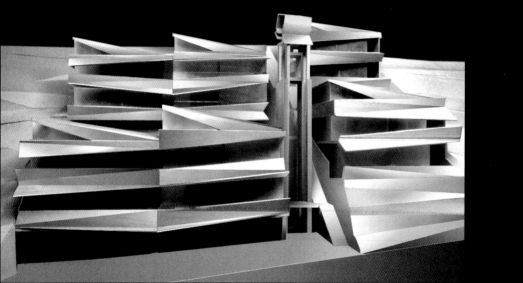

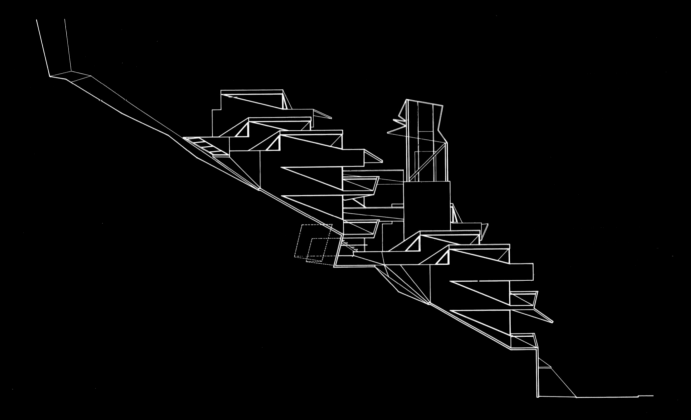

Six Housing Units, Brig

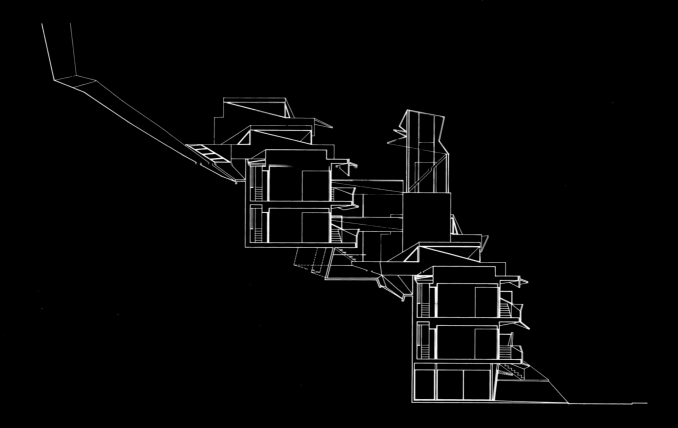

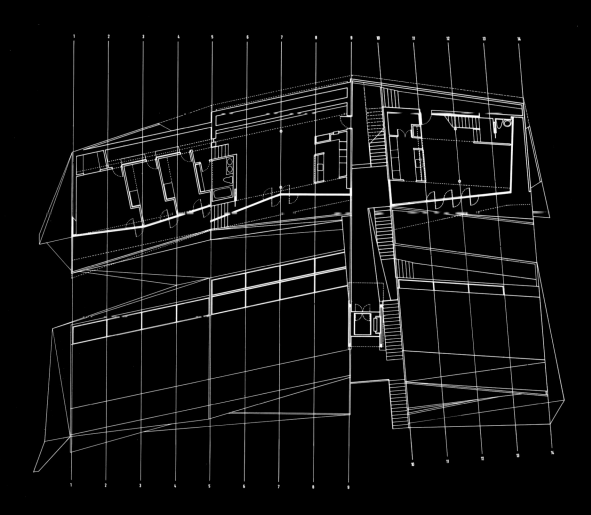

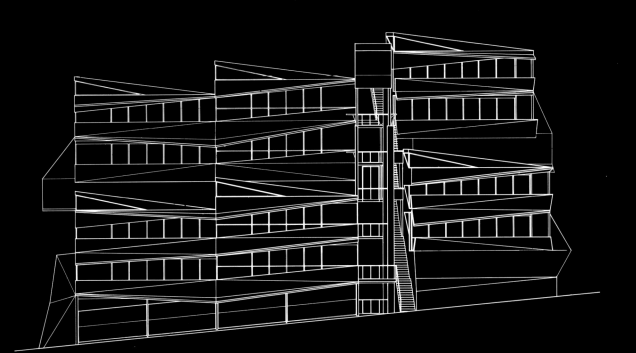

The Groningen Courthouse is an architecture that reestablishes the public institution as a place of event and engagement. This scheme challenges notions of elitism and resists the conventional tendency to conceive of public buildings as hierarchical and monumental; at the same time, it assumes a skepticism toward the authoritarian and highly bureaucratic programmatic brief. Another essential consideration in this proposal was the prominent political and public profile of the Courthouse in the city of Groningen and in the Netherlands.

Given that the groundlevel here had been artificially determined, the site was emptied and filled conceptually through a process of imprinting and stamping. Elements were inserted into a new ground plane as game pieces on an ordered, clearly delineated field. The resulting minimalist canvas yielded two datums, one at 22.5 meters above grade and another at 3.5 meters below grade. The upper datum functioned as an inverse ground plane while the subgrade datum implied an inverted roofline. The bases of the various courthouse structures thus redefined the ground plane as an articulated assemblage of buildings while the actual roofline remained devoid of embellishment and formal articulation. The subgrade datum, an extension of the urban square fronting the site, forms an inclined plaza beneath the cantilevered buildings. This transition between the courthouse and the square, delineated by a row of lifted volumes, allows public access through and around the complex. Here the fleeting activity of in-line skaters, cyclists, and skateboarders carves yet another architecture beneath these totems to tedium and order.

The most public area in the complex is the visitors hall, a rectangular glass prism cantilevered over the adjacent public square, extending beyond the property line into the space of the city. One enters the courthouse not by ascending a monumental grand stair or moving through an embellished portal, but by slipping beneath a hovering glass volume into a modestly scaled space. This entry leads to the public hall, an elevated, light-filled interior spanning the length of the site. In contrast to the utilitarian corridors that constitute the typically banal public space of courthouses, the hall is an overscaled and disproportionate space emphasizing the public aspect of the judicial process. This space contains large projection screens for closed-circuit broadcasts of ongoing court proceedings, mounted high above the waiting area, security control booths with an array of surveillance monitors, and public areas with telephones, fax machines, and computer terminals with modems. Here one may observe a constant flow of individuals traversing the structure on ramps that lead up to the adjacent courtrooms; this activity charges the space with an urgent vitality and an impending sense of the unpredictable.

A large structure sheathed in a taut black translucent skin houses the courtrooms, private chambers, and antechambers. As viewed from the exterior, its skeletal structure evokes a blurred and imprecise world; from within the courtrooms, views of the city are transformed, as if seen through night vision goggles that make even the most mundane subjects appear uncanny and dangerous. Buildings containing offices and ancillary services lie parallel across the remaining area of the site. These opaque volumes with notated metal surfaces contrast with the massive seamless courtroom structure and the transparent prism of the visitors hall.

Here the interplay between autonomous structure and uniform field yields an architecture at once accessible and impenetrable, alluding to the paradoxical nature of policy making and judicial practice, in which one arrives at reconciliation only through a tedious and often static bureaucratic process.

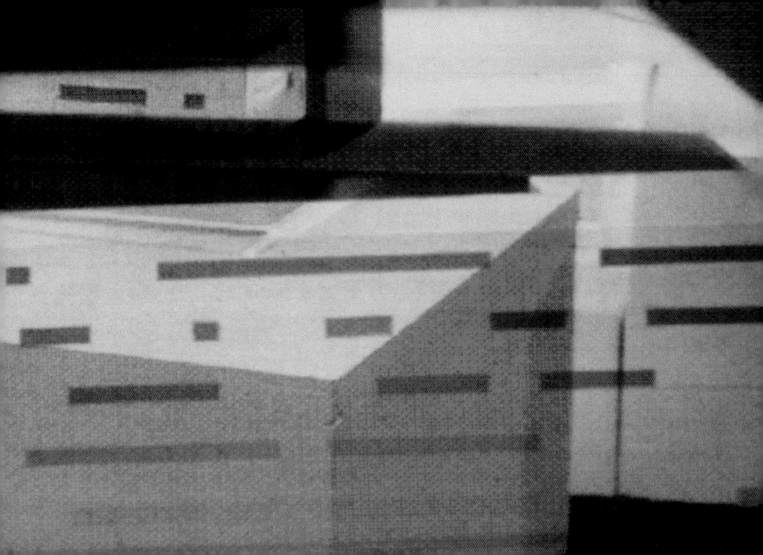

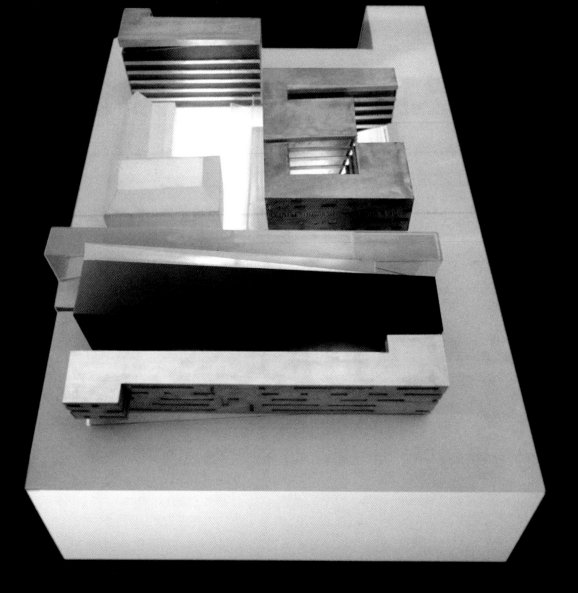

Groningen Courthouse

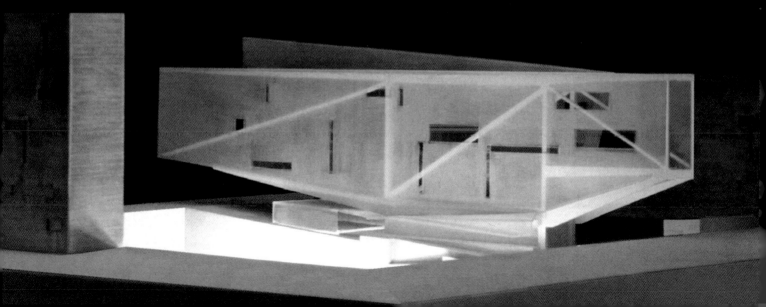

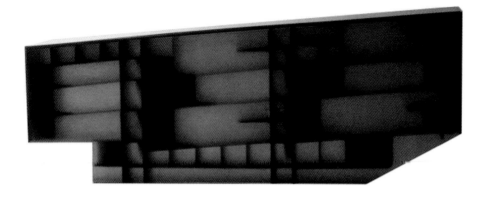

Berlin is at a critical juncture in its history: the Wall has been razed and newborn fears and nationalist sentiments have surfaced. Caught between its irreconcilable past and the desire for an untainted future, Berlin held an international competition for the design of a new parliamentary precinct within the city's reunited territories.

Motivated primarily by political strategies rather than social agendas or urban ideals, the city selected a site with an illustrious and somewhat dubious past. Here in the Spreebogen, the Berlin Wall and the Reichstag, the seat of power for Germany's pre—World War II government, coexisted for thirty years. It is a site that formerly straddled East Berlin and West Berlin, until the Wall finally collapsed on November 9, 1989. Since this event the Wall has been systematically dismantled, marketed, and commodified. This recent history and its effects compelled this scheme, one that overtly contradicts notions of repair and replacement that would effectively eradicate history and memory.

The field studies by Piet Mondrian, Paul Klee, and Keith Haring, and the prodigious works of countless anonymous graffiti artists who systematically covered the western surface of the Wall, were instrumental in the methodical deployment of a possible architecture for this site. A textual and notational resurfacing is evident in the meandering tectonics of this scheme, whose contorted morphologies engendered the plan. A systematic calligraphic process revealed inadvertent locations for building, alleviating the need to clear the land entirely and fill in the last remaining traces of its history. This plan is ultimately a *score* for a city grappling with the irreversibility and potency of history.

Within this urban proposal are four distinct territories:

1. At the northern part of the site, along the U-Bahn and S-Bahn rail lines, various structures are connected to the city fabric through their morphological similarity and program.

2. Buildings dedicated to parliamentary functions lie in another east-west band across the site. A new street and tram line bisect this area, bringing the city's vitality and activity into and through the entire zone.

3. The Spree river meanders through an eighty-meter-wide park that links the Tiergarten to the new parliamentary precinct on one side while serving as a portal to the city on the other.

4. The former Platz der Republik here is transformed into a new plaza with exaggerated proportions. Its surface slopes at a six-degree angle relative to the horizon, beginning four meters above grade opposite the Reichstag and terminating three meters below grade at the western edge of the site, adjacent to the Kongresshalle.

The two structures housing the major German governmental bodies, the Bundesrat and the Bundestag, face each other across the inclined plaza. Viewed from the Bundesrat across this five-hundred-meter-long expanse, the Reichstag appears severed at midsection. This disjunctive structure and others in the scheme suggest dislocation and recombination, reinforcing the notion that the Berlin parliament complex is a site of accountability and fallibility.

Also significant is a tract of manicured park along a minor axis that traverses the site from north to south. From an elevated position adjacent to the Soviet Memorial this park descends to the edge of the Spree and continues on the opposite bank, physically connecting the Tiergarten with the river and city beyond.

To the north, across the Spree, are sites designated for the Federal Press Conference Center, the Press Club, and a hotel. These structures would be directly adjacent to the proposed U-Bahn and S-Bahn stations, thereby creating a vital link to the city at large. The proposal also includes two new structures for the infamous "Dead Zone" or "No Man's Land," an area that for three decades separated East Berlin from West Berlin. The proposed buildings would house various creative and artistic enterprises that provide a forum for the diverse points of view that were formerly suppressed. The presence of an underground museum dedicated to the history of the Berlin Wall is marked only by an incision on the site, a glass-surfaced walkway that traces the immutable location of the former Wall. This etched line, an aperture into the museum below, is perceived at night as a thread of light meandering across the emptiness.

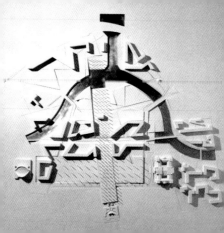

Parliamentary Precinct, Berlin Spreebogen

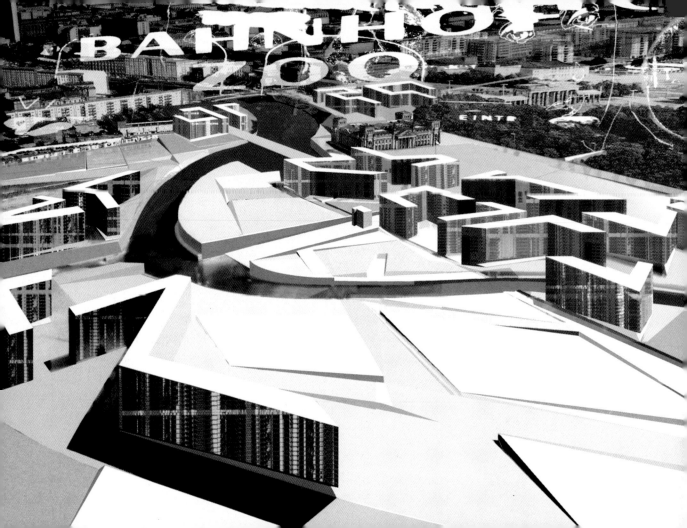

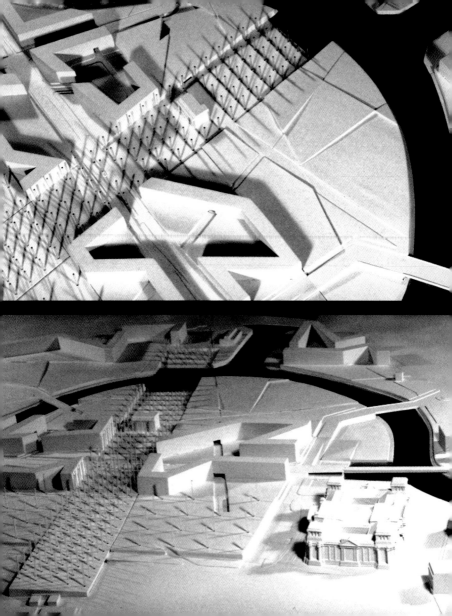

Local politicians and cultural groups in the city of Tours invited ten international architectural firms to compete for the design of new facilities for contemporary art and an addition to an existing music conservatory to house a new concert hall and performance theater. The site, the cloistered space of a former medieval convent currently occupied by the National Conservatory of Music, has become a new public domain within the density of Tours's medieval quarter. Here at the center of a formerly private enclave, a new public garden becomes the focal point not only for these facilities but also for the various historical monuments and cultural institutions in the surrounding urban area.

This public space takes the form of a landscaped plinth that connects the two new facilities across the site. One facility is for viewing and displaying art; another is for theater and performance. Here the programs for the new buildings are defined either by the outcome of performing (making art) or by the art of performing (outcome). The plinth between them offers a place for contemplation and retreat amid the ambient, dissonant sounds of instruments tuning and repeating musical scales.

From within this public space and the vantage point of the galleries, the theater appears as a massive volume rising from beneath the plinth. A translucent glass enclosure obscures a barely discernible, large, distorted white cube that houses the stage area of the theater. Here the dramatic and musical activity is rendered mute; yet the minimalist facades are animated by the silhouettes of stage props and theater machines, while a mysterious quality of light emanates from the space within. The main hall of the theater projects toward the city and is suspended above the glass-enclosed entrance. The audience itself becomes a spectacle as the sunken lobby, visible from the street, constantly fills and empties with patrons during intermissions, galas, and pre-theater festivities.

In contrast to the theater, the interior space of the contemporary art center is framed by a single tall window that is extruded from the gallery interior and protrudes toward the street, affording passersby a distorted view of the gallery's contents. This overt gesture brings the space of the gallery into the realm of the city and reveals the interior of an institution too often perceived as private and elitist. One of two ramps ascends alongside this extruded space and leads directly into the gallery, while the other descends to the public space of the plinth.

These architectural interventions evolved from a program concerned on the one hand with creating art, and on the other with the effects of public reaction. This architecture invites participation in the sometimes strange rites of artistic production and the dissemination of art. In this place of impromptu encounters, art openings, rehearsals, and happenings, the products and labors of the artist and the inherent contradictions in the promotion of culture are disclosed and subverted.

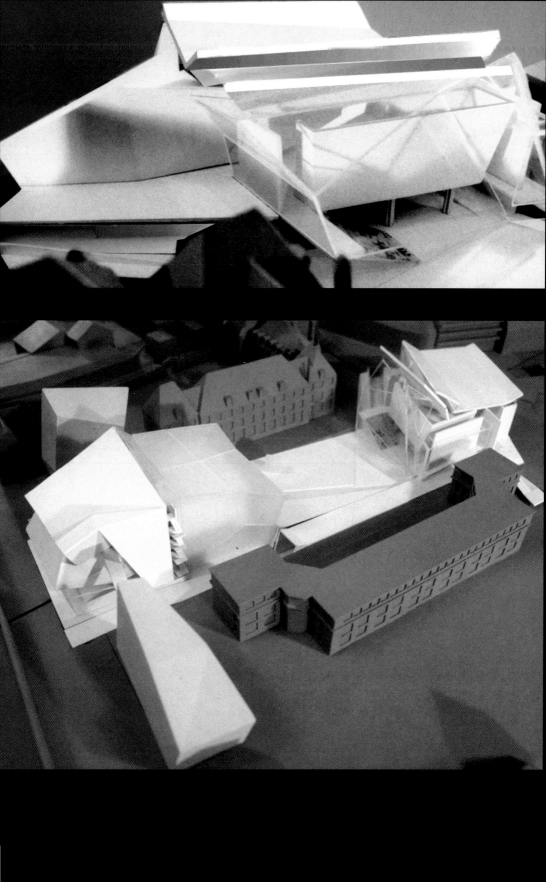

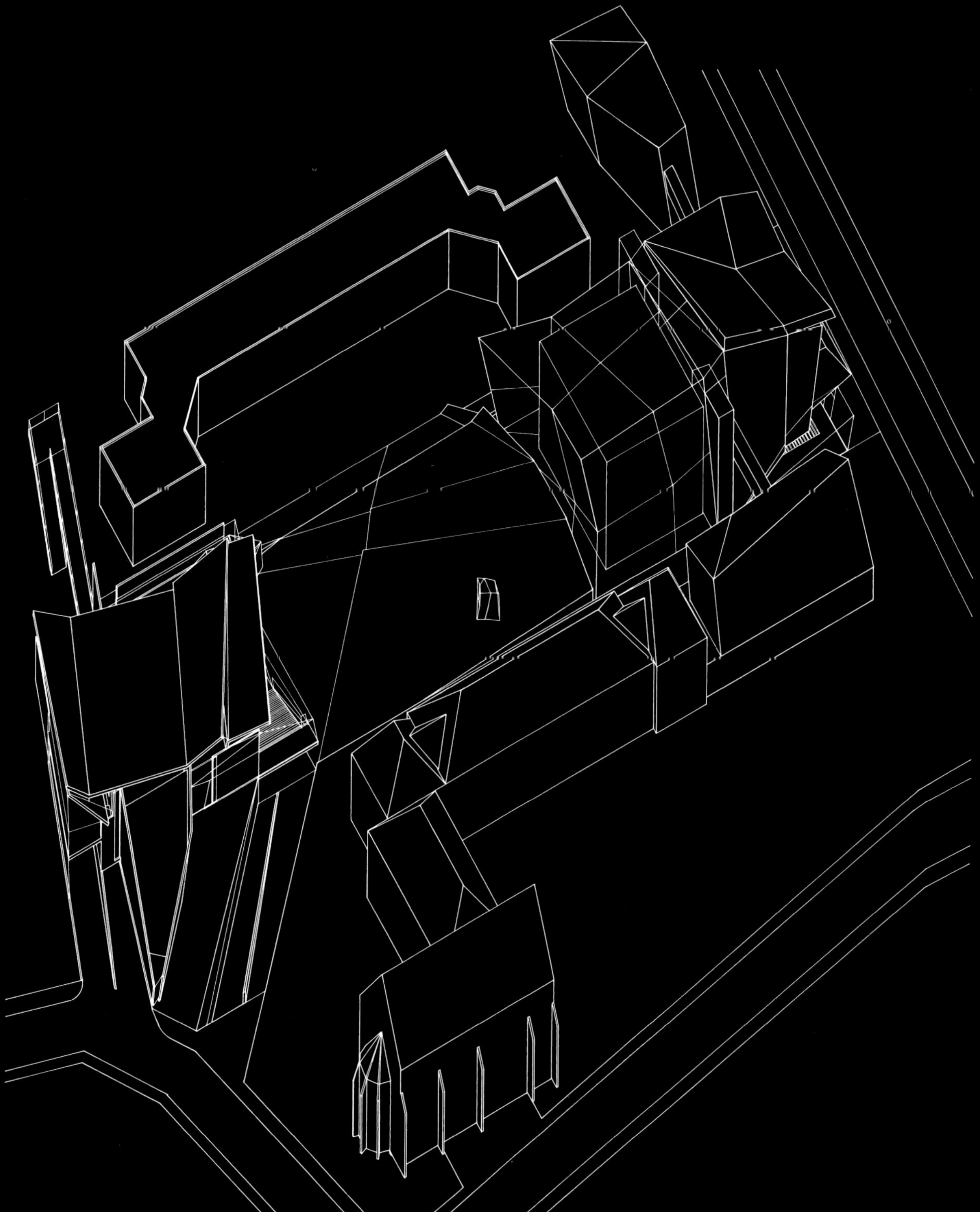

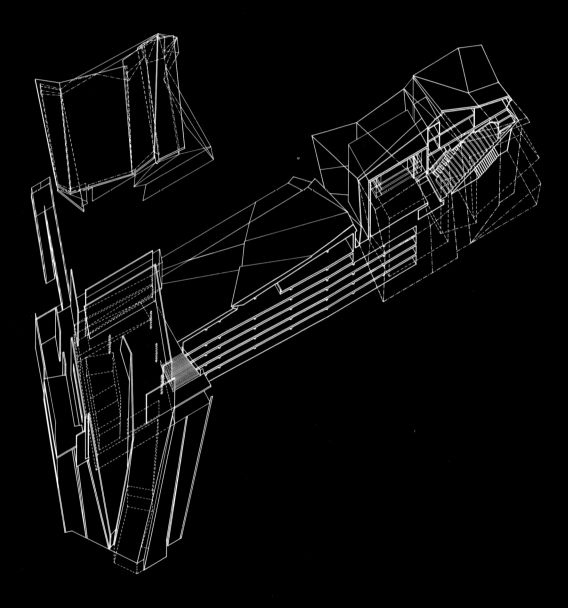

Center for Contemporary Culture, Tours

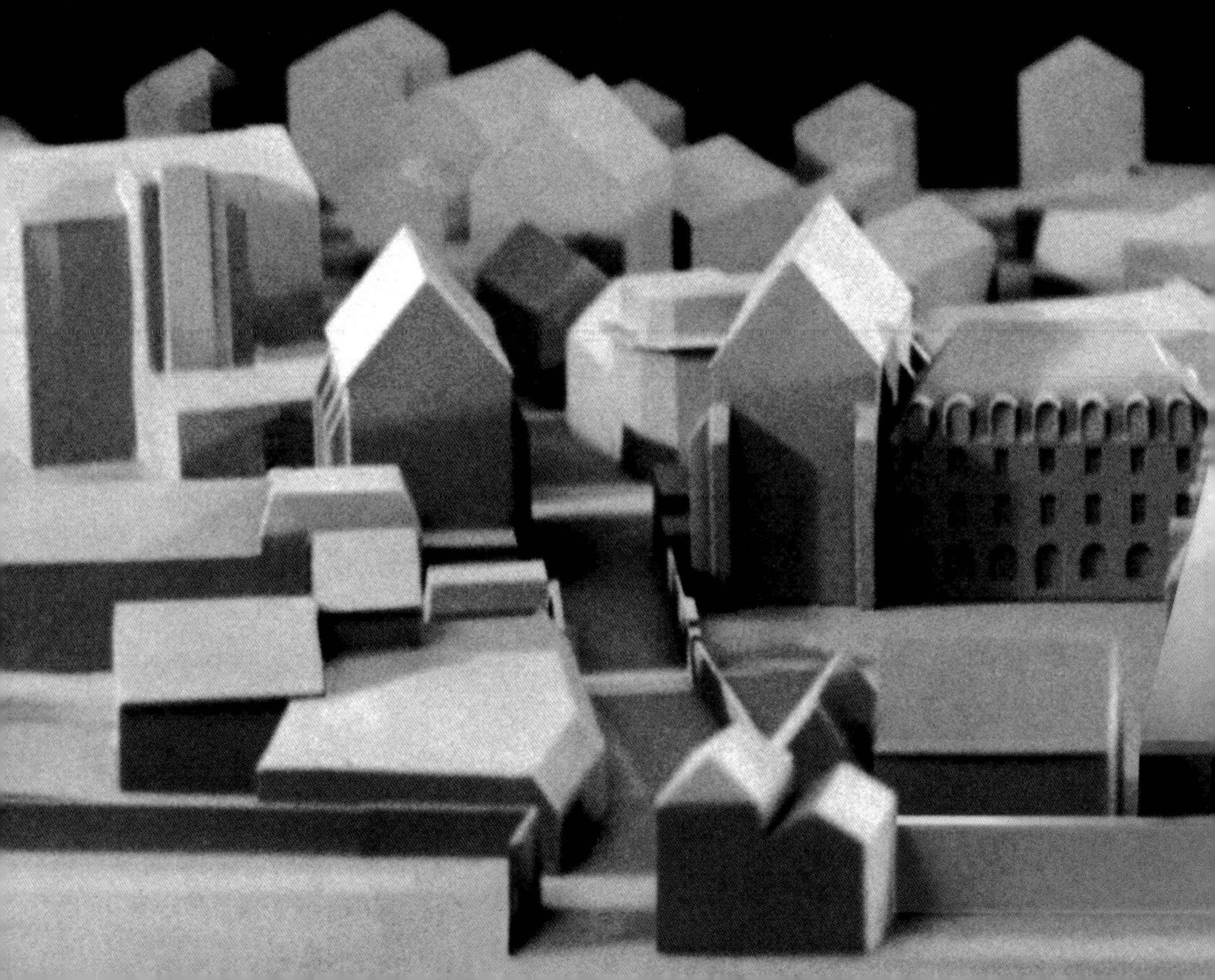

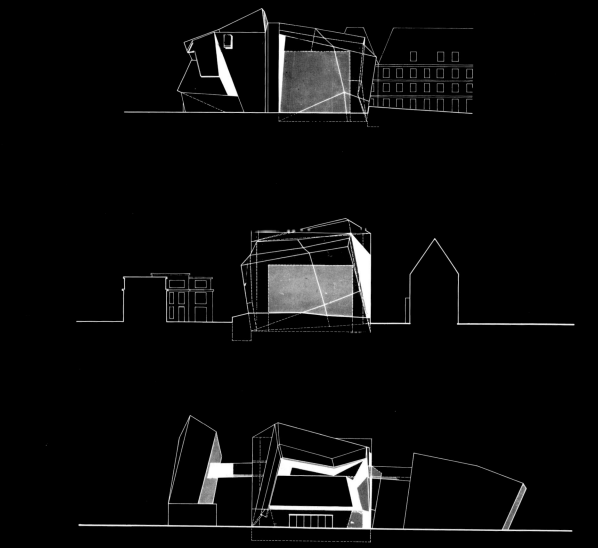

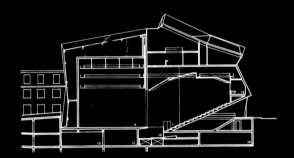

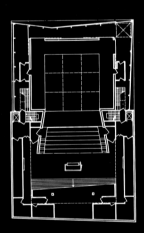
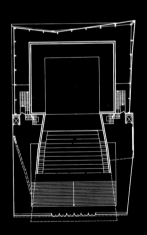
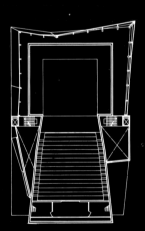

Center for Contemporary Culture, Tours

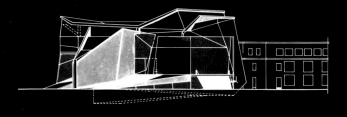

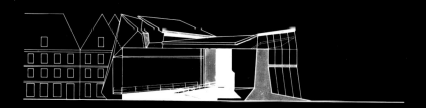

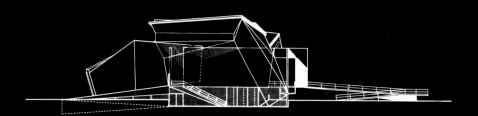

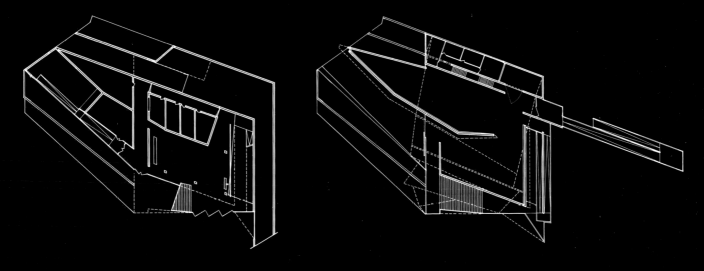

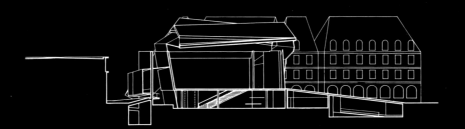

Center for Contemporary Culture, Tours

This proposed museum outside the city of Sendai in Tohoku prefecture focuses didactically on the region's agrarian-based cultural heritage. These exhibition spaces house artifacts that illuminate and evoke the traditions and rituals as well as the myths and narratives that continue to evolve along with a rich history of rice cultivation.

Tohoku today is experiencing considerable social, political, and geographical change. Younger generations of Japanese in this area increasingly value nonagrarian forms of production and manufactured commodities, particularly electronics and high-technology goods. The museum occupies a site where encroaching suburbs, the tracks of the Tokyo-bound bullet train, and expanding highways are quickly obliterating any physical evidence of the area's colorful history.

The museum is to occupy a flat, nondescript site that for centuries had been devoted exclusively to rice farming. Faint traces of this former activity exist on the terrain in the form of linear demarcations that once represented land divisions and ownership. The scheme's organization is contingent upon the elusive presence of these residual incisions and scars, marks of a time when the fields were seeded, flooded, and cultivated.

Two existing irrigation canals serve as organizational devices for this scheme and as the main avenues of public circulation. Glass-enclosed passageways with transparent floors laid above these canals overlook a variety of garden spaces and lead to the various exhibit halls. These passageways terminate at a large wall-like structure that borders the site to the north and west. Housed within are the nonpublic aspects of the program—administrative offices, research laboratories, archives, and vast storage facilities. The sloping profiles of this wall-like element serve as a backdrop to the remaining museum structures and constitute a barrier to the adjacent highway and tracks of the bullet train. From the vantage point of a moving train or car the museum complex is momentarily visible only when the inclined roof passes beneath eye level. The interior courtyards formed between the wall-like element and other museum components frame traditional landscapes in a diorama-like manner.

Traces of speed and modernity permeate the site in the form of reflections of the trains and cars on glass surfaces that overlook the gardens; the inclined and bellowed roofs of the various pavilions, on the other hand, are a deliberate abstraction of traditional and sacred Japanese forms. This juxtaposition of contemporary and traditional elements emphasizes the fact that in many ways the museum embodies a constructed history. As one meanders through this museum, one abandons subtle distinctions between past and present, real and fabricated.

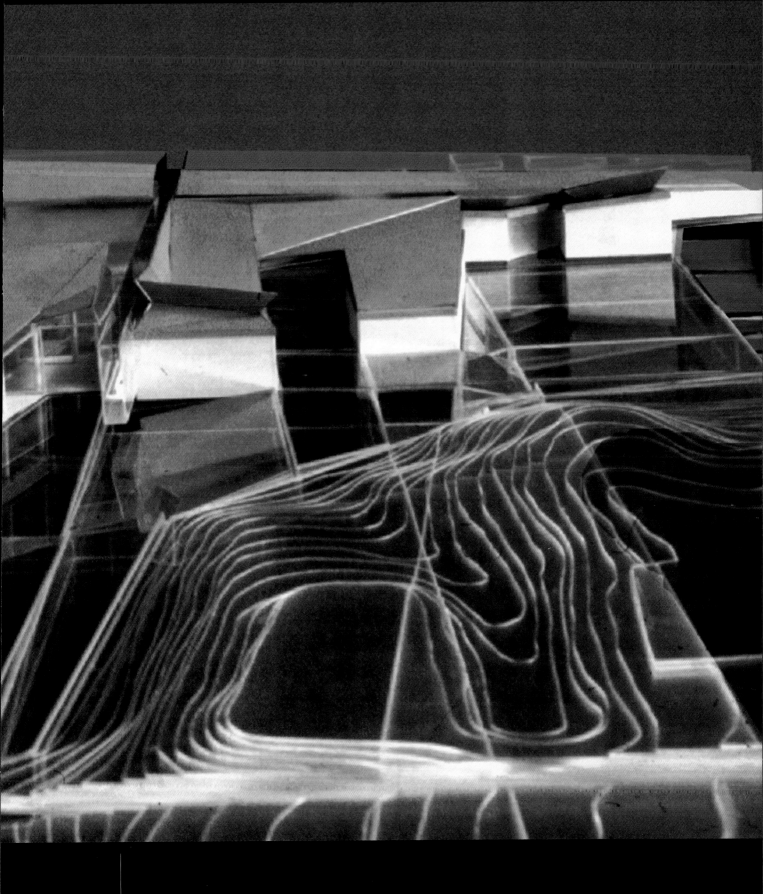

Tohoku Historical Museum

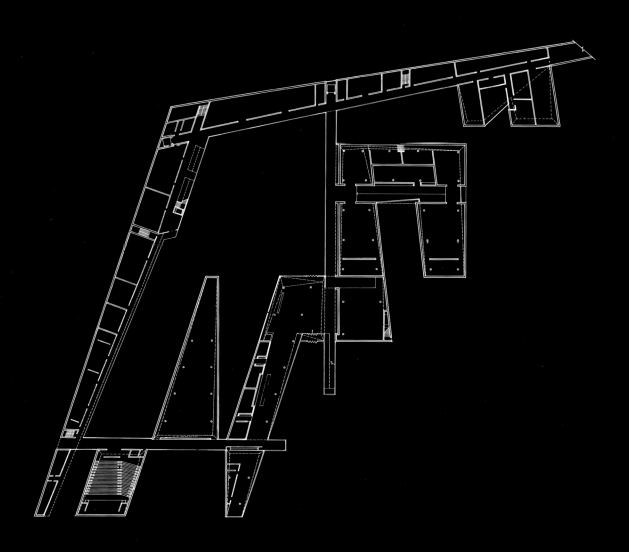

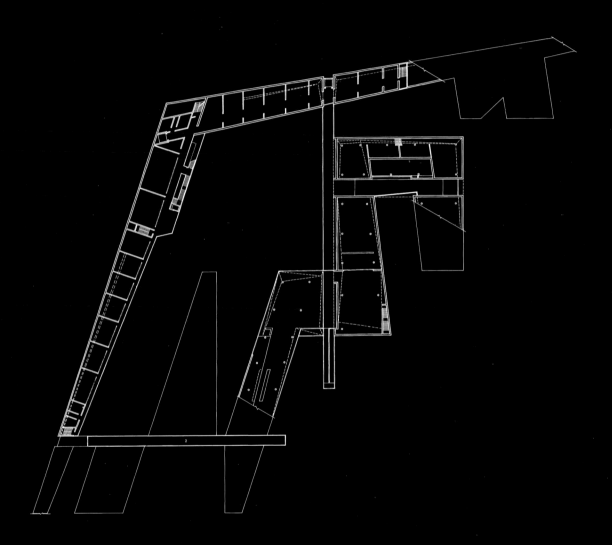

Tohoku Historical Museum

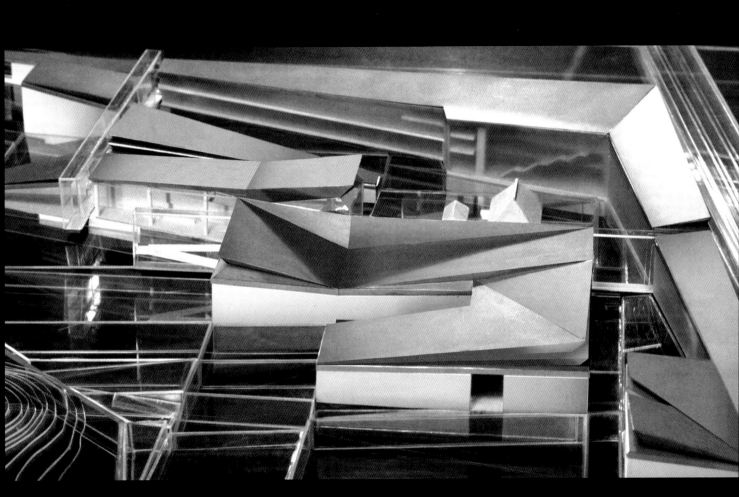

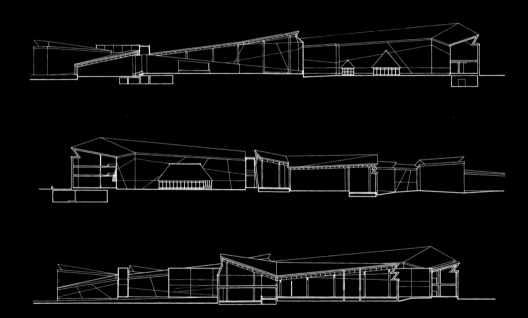

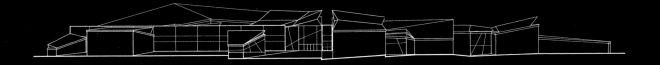

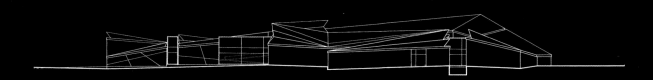

Tohoku Historical Museum

In this proposal the Yokohama Passenger Ship Terminal projects three distinct identities: an international gateway to Japan, an extension of the city of Yokohama into the bay, and a unique public place inviting curiosity, desire, anticipation, and abandon. The new terminal serves as a point of entry to the city, efficiently fulfilling the requisite processing functions associated with passengers and cargo, yet also embracing the delirium that tourism and escape inspire. This is a structure and a place for *those who arrive, those who stay,* and *those who depart.*

Arrival

The strange and ethereal appearance of land at a distant shoreline is a phenomenon unique to sea travel. From the vantage point of a ship the city appears indiscernible and enigmatic, making the experience of arriving one of awe and amazement. The terminal is to be viewed and experienced from beneath the Bay Bridge during the approach into the port of Yokohama. It is a vivid sight against the backdrop of the city: taut volumes embedded in the lifted horizon lines of a tethered structure that seems momentarily held from floating out to sea. This facility addresses the twenty-first century through its spirit of mutability within a fluctuating context. The architecture forms against the shoreline as an abstraction of the movement of liquids; its geometry evolved from concepts of erosion, fusion, and coalescence. It is a structure inspired by the movement of a ship's propeller, or the mast of a sail filling with wind.

Staying

As a ship approaches the terminal it appears to slip on the surface of the water beneath the distant bridge. The vessel's scale and position shift slowly upon its approach; in a few moments its mammoth hull attaches slowly to the side of the building. The interior spaces of the terminal are now temporarily complete: the alternating presence and frequent absence of ships are crucial to the formation of this architecture. The terminal is also a public thoroughfare, a prosthetic to the city's edge. Horizontal decks, roofs, and passageways form a suspended landscape that spans the entire length of the terminal. This public facility is always open and accessible, a place where visitors, onlookers, sightseers, courting couples, lamenting souls, and aficionados of ships, ports, and navigation meander freely. To experience this architecture is to be made vividly aware of the surroundings, the sea, the strange and ephemeral light, and the odd scents and staccato sounds that float across the bay and terminal.

Departure

A long ramp rises gradually from the sanctuary of the city to meet an inclined, half-submerged, enigmatic glass volume enclosing the departure and arrival hall. The city and harbor seem increasingly distant with each step toward the illuminated volume, and upon entering the departure hall one soon leaves behind any sense of yearning or nostalgia. Here a flurry of activity— ticketing, porters quickly moving to and fro, and luggage whirling by—is accompanied by video images of far-off places appearing on large screens suspended above. These distracting activities and seductive images turn the mind away from the angst of departure. Beyond the walls of glass encircling the departure hall the city of Yokohama now seems a surreal backdrop. Inside, the intersecting paths of arriving and departing passengers instill a deeper sense of adventure and anticipation. Glancing down from the waiting room suspended above the hall to the random activity below, one realizes that the journey is well on its way.

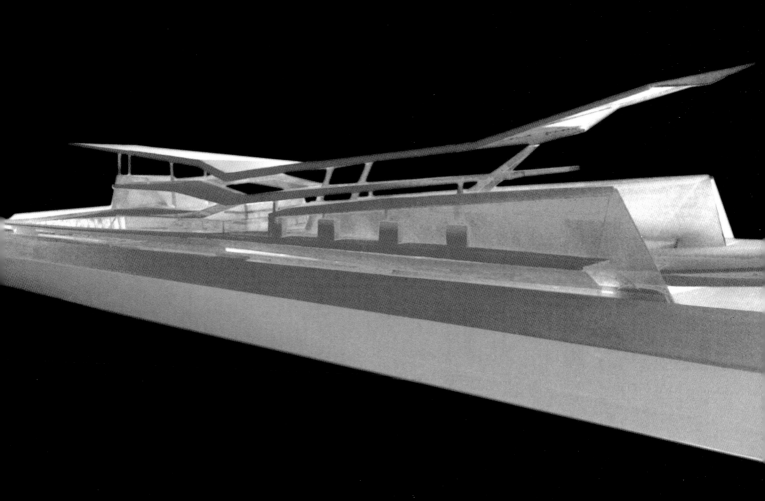

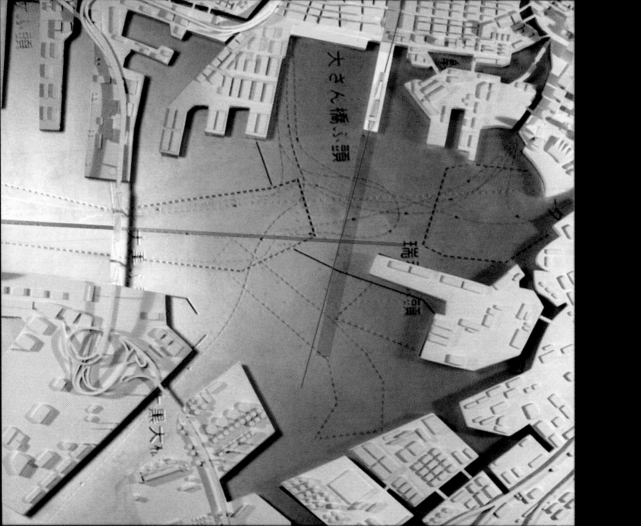

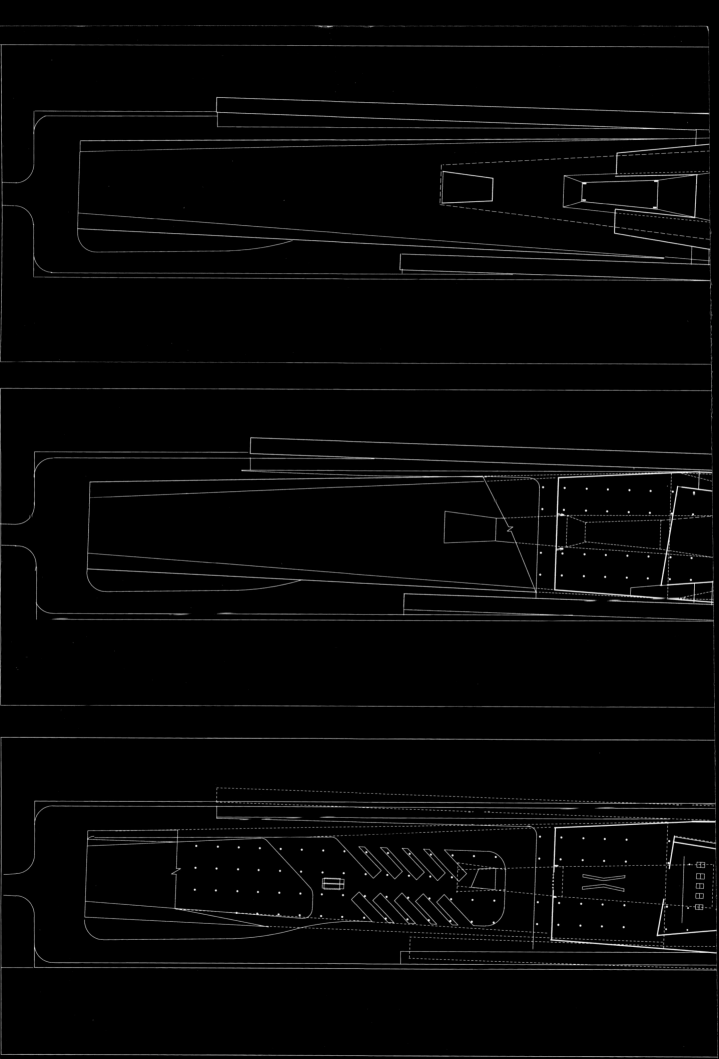

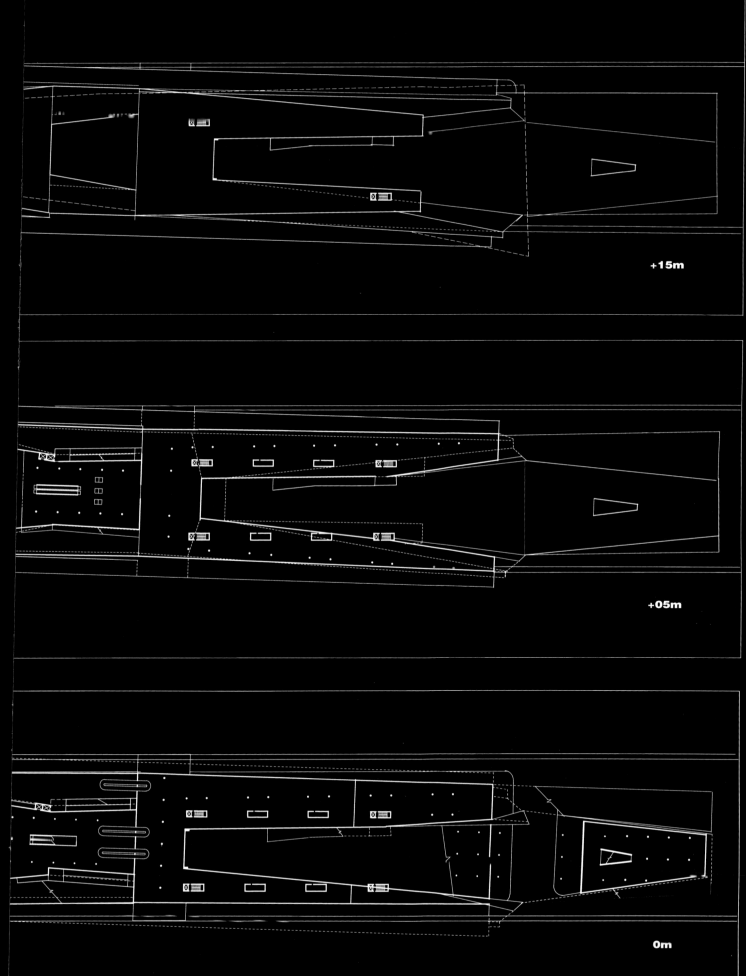

+15m

+05m

0m

Yokohama Passenger Ship Terminal

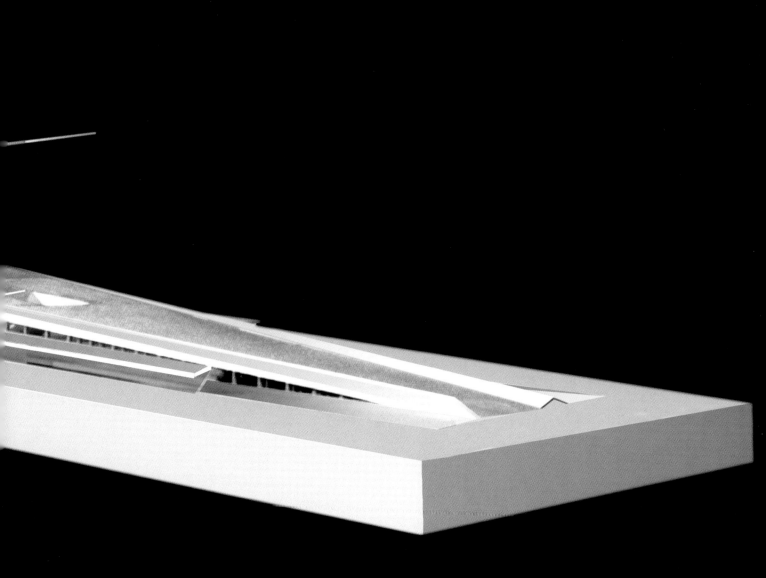

Yokohama Passenger Ship Terminal

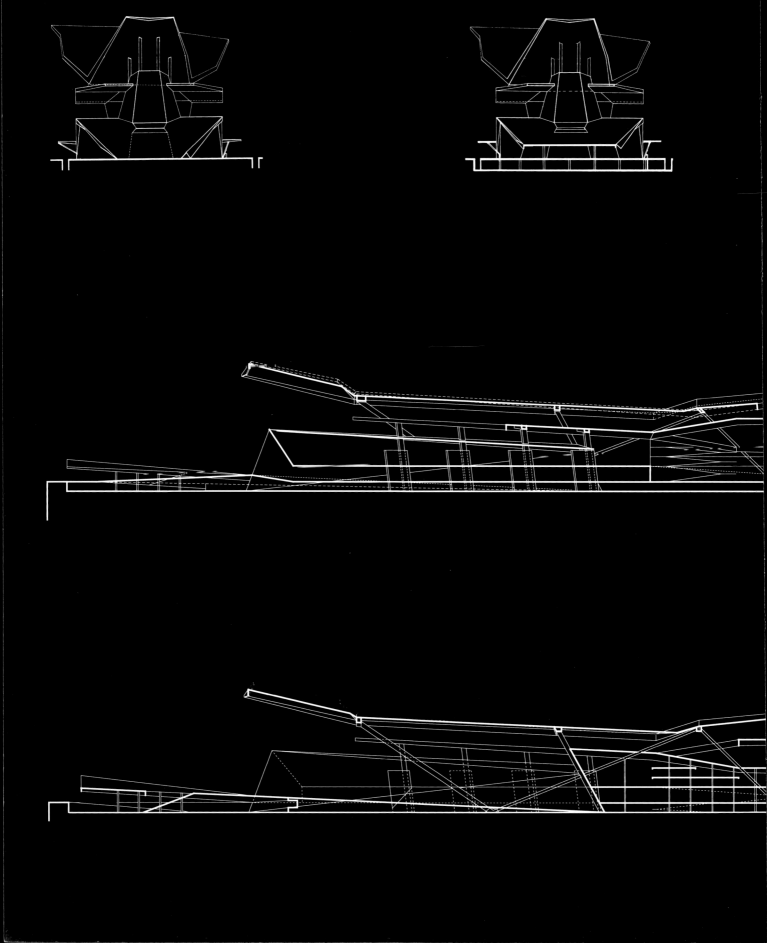

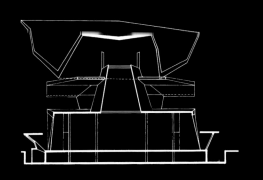

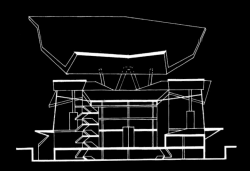

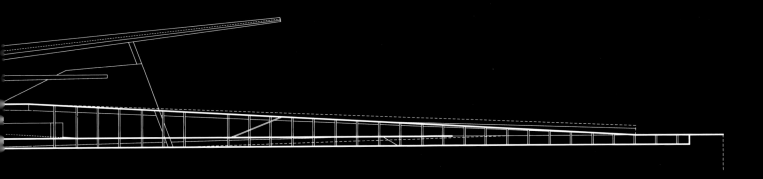

Yokohama Passenger Ship Terminal

EXHIBITIONS

Canadian Centre for Architecture, Montréal, Canada, "Urban Revisions," September - October 1994.

Grand Hall, Takashimaya, Kyoto, Japan, "Asymptote: Ten Projects," September 1994.

Uzzan Galerie, Paris, France, "Hyperfine Splitting," June 1994.

Museum of Contemporary Art, Los Angeles, California, "Urban Revisions," May 1994.

Centre de Création Contemporain, Tours, France, "L'architecte est sur les lieux," April 1994.

Musée des Beaux Arts, Chartres, France, Group Show, February 1994.

German Cultural Center, New York, New York, "Berlin: Designing a Capital for the 21st Century," September 1993.

Avery Hall, Columbia University, New York, New York, "Berlin Spreebogen Competition," June 1993.

Whiteley's, London, England, "Theory & Experimentation," June 1992.

Sadock & Uzzan Galerie, Paris, France, "Les Architectes Plasticiens," February 1991.

Architecture Gallery, Princeton University, Princeton, New Jersey, "Anaglyptic Architecture," December 1990.

Buell Hall, Columbia University, New York, New York, "OPTIGRAPH 3," November 1990.

Fenster Gallery, Frankfurt, Germany, "ASYMPTOTE," November 1990.

UNESCO Headquarters, Paris, France, "Alexandria Library Finalists," November 1990.

Staatliche Kunsthalle, Berlin, Germany, "Paris—Architektur und Utopie," July 1990.

Anna Leonowens Gallery, Halifax, Nova Scotia, Canada, "Asymptote," June 1990.

Aedes Gallery, Berlin, Germany, "Experimental Architecture," February 1990.

Pacific Design Center, Los Angeles, California, "West Coast Gateway," March 1990

Emily Carr Gallery, Vancouver, Canada "Rashid+Rashid," January 1990.

Pavilion de l'Arsenal, Paris, France, "Paris—Thought Pattern for the 21st Century," November 1990.

Gallery 76, Toronto, Canada, "Theory and Practice," November 1989.

Steelcase Gallery, New York, New York, "30 under 30," October 1989.

Griffith McGear Gallery, New York, New York "Form, Being; Absence," May 1989.

2AES, San Francisco, California, "The Steel Cloud," April 1989.

Artists Space, New York, New York, "Kursaal for an Evacuee," February 1988.

BIBLIOGRAPHY

1994

"Asymptote." **A+U 283** (April 1994): 47–139.

Daugaard, Morten. "Byen Under Foranding." **Arkitekten**, July 1994, 336–37.

Ferguson, Russell, ed. **Urban Revisions for the Public Realm**. Catalog, Museum of Contemporary Art, Los Angeles, (Cambridge: MIT Press, 1994), 84,152–57.

Rashid, Hani. "AGIT(N)ATION Pseudo–Architecture." **LAX: The Los Angeles Experiment**, (New York: SITES/Lumen Books, 1994), 60–67.

1993

"Analog Space to Digital Field, Asymptote Seven Projects." **Assemblage 21**:22,43.

"Aggressive Offices Created by World Architects." **Eciffo 22** (Autumn 1993): 4,7.

Amelar, Sarah. "Berlin Searches for Itself." **Metropolis**, December 1993, 42–45.

Muschamp, Herbert. "Berlin, Designing a Capital for the 21st Century." **New York Times**, October 15, 1993, C36.

Papadakis, Andreas. "Asymptote." **Theory + Experimentation**, (London: Academy Editions, 1993), 48,110–19.

1992

"Asymptote." **Semiotext(e)**, Fall 1992, 15–21.

"ASYMPTOTE / Hani Rashid and Lise Anne Couture." **SD, Space Design 336** (September 1992): 62,67.

"Teatro estatal de Moscu." **Arquitectura 6** (Summer 1992): 46–47.

Gubitosi, Alessandro. "Nube d'acciaio." **l'ARCA 66**:74–79.

Muschamp, Herbert. "Time to Reset the Clock in Times Square." **New York Times**, November 1, 1992, Arts & Leisure, 1.

Rashid, Hani. "Meditations on Architecture in a Media Field." **Pratt Journal 3: On Making**, 198–203.

1991

"Nuage d'acier." **Technique & Architecture 394** (February/March 1991): 102–105.

Cook, Peter and Rosie Llewellyn-Jones. **New Spirit In Architecture**, (New York: Rizzoli International Publications, Inc., 1991), 132–35.

Levesque, Luc. "L'amonument pour l'Amerique a l'aube du 21e siècle." **Inter Art Actuel 51**:64–65.

Phillips, Patricia. "Reviews." **ARTFORUM**, February 1991, 128.

Rashid, Hani. "Optigraphs and Other Writings." In **Architectural Design Profile 89**, (London: Academy Editions, 1991), 86–91.

Shane, Grahame. "Neue Zentrum für Los Angeles." **Archithese**, January–February 1991, 74–75.

Wagner, Sebastian. "Utopica, eine Europäische Idee." **Bauwelt 21** (June 1991): 1066.

1990

"Deconstruction 3." **Architectural Design Profile 87**, (London: Academy Editions, 1990), 52, 58, 61.

"Three Projects by Studio Asymptote." **A+U 241**:38–39.

"Wettbewerb West Coast Gateway, Los Angeles, 1988." **Werk, Bauen+Wohen**, July–August 1990, 19.

Danese, Sylvia and Benedetta Tagliabue. "LA, Gate." **Utopica 4**:25–29.

Pallasmaa, Juhani. "Deconstruction of a Monument." **Arkkitehti 3**:79–83.

Rashid, Hani and Lise Anne Couture. "OPTIGRAPH 2." In **RIEA, The First Conference**, (New York: Princeton Architectural Press, 1990).

Rashid, Hani and Lise Anne Couture. **Optigraph 3: Berlin Readouts**, Miniseries 3, (New York: Columbia University Graduate School of Architecture, Planning and Preservation, 1990).

1989

"Asymptote." **A+U 231** (December 1989): 5–28.

"Californians Are Talking." **Newsweek**, June 12, 1989, 6.

"Competition: Los Angles West Coast Gateway." **Plus / Architecture + Interior Design 23**:154–59.

"Front Page." **Art In America**, February 1989, 21.

"News." **Architectural Record**, February 1989, 71.

"P/A News." **Progressive Architecture**, February 1989, 22–23.

"Steel Cloud." **Architecture Cree 232** (November 1989): 19.

Giovannini, Joseph. "Key to the City, A Healing Arch." **Metropolitan Home**, August 1989, 40–42.

Heintz, John. "A Building Called Steel Cloud." **VOX**, April 1989, 8–10.

Holt, Steven. "New York." **AXIS 33** (Autumn 1989): 19.

Muschamp, Herbert. "Ground Up." **ARTFORUM**, September 1989, 14–15.

Nesbitt, Kate. "West Coast Gateway." **SKALA 17/18**:28–29.

Rashid, Hani. "On Recent Non-Events." In **Architecture and Utopia**, (Berlin: Ernst & Sohn, 1989), 166–67.

Schwartzman, Alan. "Monumental Trouble." **ELLE**, September 1989, 14–15.

Smith, Richard. "Artnotes." **New Art Examiner 6** (February 1989): 72.

Starr, Kevin. "An Urban Dream." **Image**, August 13, 1989, 17, 23.

Woods, Lebbeus. "Experimental Architecture, A Commentary." **Avant Garde 2**:12.

1988

"Monumental Folly." **TIME**, December 19, 1988, 30.

CREDITS

Principal architects: Hani Rashid, Lise Anne Couture

Lanciano Urban Plan, 1988
Dale Corvino, Thomas Han, Ignacio Salas

Los Angeles West Coast Gateway: The Steel Cloud, 1988
Jocelyne Beaudoin, Raoul Bustos, Richard Cress, Begonia Fernandez-Shaw, Wissam Jabr, Eytan Kaufman, Ursula Kurz, Michelle Lederer, Marisable Marratt, Nuno Mateus, Ignacio Salas, Mark Wamble, Christopher Warnick, Beth Weinstein

Alexandria Library, 1989
John Cleater, David Currie, Scott Devere, Philip Teft, Diane Kramer, Ursula Kurz, Mark Wamble, Beth Weinstein

Moscow State Theater, 1990
In collaboration with Thomas Leeser Architecture, New York
John Cleater, David Currie, Felicia Davis, Michelle Lederer, Ignacio Salas, Sylvain Vallot, Lee Washesky, Beth Weinstein

Groningen Courthouse, 1991
In collaboration with Wiel Arets & Associates, Heerlen, the Netherlands
John Cleater, William Deegan, Scott Devere, Kevin Estrada, Marianne Geers

Six Housing Units, Brig, 1992
In collaboration with Mateja Vehovar, Zurich, Switzerland
Kevin Estrada

Parliamentary Precinct: Berlin Spreebogen, 1992
Kevin Estrada, Helen Ferguson, Omar Kahn, Brian Messana, Marguerite Montecinos, Sherri Olsen, Ignacio Salas

Center for Contemporary Culture, Tours, 1993
In association with Fabienne Bulle and Jean Michel Brinon Architects, Paris, France
Dubravka Antic, Kimberly Bassett, Kevin Estrada, Christoph Kaltenbrunner, Frederik Svenstedt, Eric Worcester

Tohoku Historical Museum, 1994
In association with Yasui Hideo Atelier, Tokyo, Japan
Joseph Bula, Kevin Estrada, Howon Kang, Nadine Nakasha, Kazuko Sakamoto, Frederik Svenstedt, Eric Worcester, Linda Lu

Yokohama Passenger Ship Terminal, 1994
William Deegan, Kevin Estrada, Jeffrey Johnson, Diogo S. Lopes, Paolo Lopes, Lynne Miyamoto, Max Müller, Ryuichi Sasaki

Photography: Eduard Hueber (p. 69, pp. 72–73, pp. 79–80, p. 91, p. 95, p. 116, p. 145); Douglas Whyte (pp. 60–67, p. 75)

Rizzoli International Publications, New York: David A. Morton, Senior Editor, Architecture; Elizabeth White, Managing Editor; Megan McFarland, Assistant Editor, Architecture; Belinda Hellinger, Production Associate

Produced digitally at **Asymptote**, New York